LAURA'S LOOK ONE HUNDRED

LAURA WARE

✾ Created with Vellum

CONTENTS

Acknowledgments   vii
Introduction   xi
A Look Back   xiii

Rambling Thoughts About 2004   1
A Look Back At 2007   5
A Look Back At 2008   7
A Look Back At 2009   9
A Look Back At 2010   13
A Look Back At 2011   15
A Look Back At 2012   19
A Look Back At 2013   23
A Look Back At 2014   25
A Look Back At 2015   29
A Look Back At 2016   31
A Look Back At 2017   33
A Look Back At 2018   35
A Look Back At 2019   39
A Look Back At 2020   41
A Look Back At 2021   45
A Look Back At 2022   49
Ripped From The Headlines   51
A New Day Of Infamy   53
Making Hay On 9/11   57
A Year After 9/11   61
A Look At The 2002 Elections   65
A Non-Fan's View Of Deflate Gate   69
A Column I Don't Want To Write   71
An Evil Day   73
Tech Got Under Her Skin   77
Boldly Going   81
Forgive This Much   85
Grandbabies   89
Welcoming A Baby   91
A Grandbaby Column   95

Their Royal Adorablenesses   97
"I Don't Know"   99
Another Grandbabies Column   101
Being Grandma   103
"Oh, Biscuits!"   105
Time With Grandbabies   109
A Hot Time With The Grandkids   111
A Grandbaby Milestone   115
Personal   119
Twenty Years   121
30 Years And Counting   123
33 Years And Counting   125
After Forty Years   127
Hanging Up The Phone On Solicitors   129
Anyone Can Have A Bad Day   133
Left Foot Right Foot   135
A Colorful Run   137
Let The Dogs Out   139
Canine Chaos   143
After Irma   147
From Couch To 5K   149
A Weighty Topic   153
Perky Crosses The Rainbow Bridge   155
A New Family Member   157
Morning People Vs. The Rest Of Us   161
The Bear Went Over The Hammock   165
I Am Strong, But I Am Tired   169
A Cut Above   171
The Further Adventures Of My Heart   175
Ups And Downs   179
A Lesson In Patience   183
Can Fat Be Useful?   187
Mom   189
To Clean Or Not To Clean   191
The Journey To A Photo   193
Travel   197
Snow, Ice, And Northern Lights   199
Hunting The Lights   203
Adventures In Traveling   207
A Trip To New York City   211

New York, New York   215
A Trip To Ohio   219
Wild Wonderful Alaska   221
Travel Tales   225
Flying After 9/11   227
A Grand Canyon   231
Two Weeks Out Of The Loop   235
Aloha!   237
More Aloha   241
The Long Way Home   245
Shore Leave   249
The Last Road Trip   253
Random Stuff   257
Being Kind   259
Carrying Our Load   263
Honk If You Hate Lovebugs   267
Christians In Name Only   271
One More Cheer For The Bucs   275
The Mystery Of The Missing Choppers   279
Being Thankful In 2020   283
Should I Chicken Out?   285
Above and Beyond   289
My Kind Of Races   291
One Particular Graduate   295
Is It A Christmas Movie?   299
Car Tales   303
Inside A Star Trek Convention   307
Flag-Waving   311
The Great Cake Caper   315
Never Judge A Book By Its Movie   319
When Good Story Meets Bad Theology   321
Dear Ann Landers   325
Those Scammy Scammers   329

Also By Laura Ware: 331
About the Author   333

ACKNOWLEDGMENTS

A number of people have played a part in bringing *Laura's Look One Hundred* to life.

Bonnie Koenig and T. Thorn Coyle were invaluable in helping me with advice regarding the Kickstarter that launched this book. Both went above and beyond the call of duty: Bonnie supplied my banner for the Kickstarter and Thorn designed the awesome cover for the book. Thanks, ladies.

Dustin McCrickard kindly and patiently helped me record a video for the Kickstarter that I could use without cringing. A busy man, he nevertheless put in the time to make it work.

As usual, Tina Seward has not only been a source of encouragement (and a beta reader to a number of these columns) but has taken the task of copyediting the manuscript. As I always say, any errors that remain are on me.

The following people took part in my Kickstarter campaign for the collection. Thank you all for believing in this project and your willingness to back it:

Carol Farmer
   Carolyn Rowland
   David H. Hendrickson
   Diana Deverell
   Jackie Dracup
   K & J
   Karen Fonville
   Leslie Claire Walker

Lisa Silverthorne
Loraine
Lorrane J. Anderson
Lyn Perry
LZ
Mary Jo Rabe
Matt Buchman
Melissa "Yi" Yuan-Innes
Michael Kingswood
Michael Warren Lucas
Pamela Cummins
Rigel Ailur
Robert Greenberger
Ryan M. Williams
Tina Seward

To Don,
For having broad enough shoulders that I can freely talk about our lives in
my columns

INTRODUCTION

Looking back, things were very different twenty-five years ago.

Cell phones were dumb. The Internet was in its infancy. Amazon was only four years old and just beginning to branch out from selling books. Netflix had just started its DVD service. Many of us had Blockbuster rental cards.

Twenty-five years ago I was a mom shepherding a nine and eleven-year-old as we tackled day-to-day living. Married fifteen years, we lived in a small rental place while our home was being built for us in Highlands County, Florida (that means my carpets are around twenty-five years old and have survived kids and dogs. Keep that in mind when you look at them).

And twenty-five years ago I began to write a column for the Highlands News-Sun. Called "Laura's Look" it first appeared in June of 1998. After going a while every other week and a brief hiatus, it became the weekly column it is today.

It has changed some since I started. After all, *I* have changed My two young sons are now grown men and one has young children of his own to guide. I am older, hopefully a little wiser, unfortunately heavier, and, I'd like to think, a better writer.

Over the years I've written over twelve hundred columns. They've covered topics from politics to stupid criminal stories, from deadly serious to silly beyond measure. All of them written from my somewhat warped point of view.

The one hundred columns included here spoke to me in one way or another. It wasn't easy narrowing the choices down. But I feel what is included is a slice of life from the past twenty-five years. And some of them may speak to you, as they spoke to me.

Some will make you laugh. A couple may make you cry. Some will make you think. All of them are included for you to enjoy, which is what I hope for whenever I send a column in to the paper. That someone out there gets something good from it.

Thanks for reading. Enjoy.

September 2023
Sebring, Florida

A LOOK BACK

*We start off with my year in review columns, a tradition I started in 2007.
These columns look back at the previous year and highlight the things that
caught my interest.*
*This section also includes a 2004 column that is similar to my later year in
review columns. It's enough like the others I felt it deserved a spot in this
section.*
So turn the page and be prepared to recall the past.

RAMBLING THOUGHTS ABOUT 2004

This week's column is devoted to some thoughts regarding the year 2004. They aren't in any particular chronological order, just written as they float to the top of my brain.

The first thing that comes up is four names. Charley. Frances. Ivan. Jeanne. All these hurricanes but Ivan (which couldn't figure out when it wasn't wanted and had the nerve to come BACK to Florida) shattered our complacency concerning Central Florida and hurricane season, not to mention shattering some roofs, fences, windows, etc.. Some of us still are repairing damage from those storms, and none of us will ever look at these storms the same way again.

Some tried to blame George Bush for the increased hurricane activity, saying that his environmental policies had brought about the conditions for these storms to thrive in. Bush got blamed for a lot of stuff this year and accused of a lot more. In the end, a majority of voters decided to keep Bush in the White House for another four years. The healing was supposed to begin when John Kerry conceded. Some of us are still waiting for the healing to occur.

One casualty of the 2004 election was Dan Rather's credibility. His decision to go ahead with a show about George Bush's National

Guard service that used questionable documents was bad enough. Sticking to his guns about it for over a week before admitting there could be a problem just made it worse. Rather should be thankful that CBS is still willing to employ him after that – but it hastened his exit from CBS News.

On the entertainment front, the Oscars made me ecstatic when "The Lord of the Rings" won 11 awards. It is a rare thing for me to agree with the choices made at the Academy Awards. In other movie news, Michael Moore made a pseudodocumentary he called "Fahrenheit 9/11" which caused a lot of controversy but changed few minds. On the other end of the spectrum Mel Gibson came out with "The Passion of the Christ" which also caused a lot of controversy but demonstrated that there was an untapped market for such movies. Chances are we will be hearing more about both films in 2005, especially when the Academy Awards are mentioned.

We said a sad and fond goodbye to Ronald Reagan, who ended his battle with Alzheimer's. We mourned the loss of Christopher Reeve, who had fought the good fight to overcome his disability to the very end. Tony Randall and Marlon Brando both passed on but live on in film and TV reruns. Yassar Arafat died in Paris, causing grief or joy depending on whether you saw him as a freedom fighter or a terrorist.

We started 2004 fighting in Afghanistan and Iraq, and we are ending the year still fighting in Afghanistan and Iraq. There were elections in Afghanistan despite fears they would not happen, and elections are still scheduled for January of 2005 in Iraq. A few soldiers proved themselves unworthy of their uniforms as pictures of their mistreatment of Iraqi prisoners hit the public.

Martha Stewart went to jail. Scott Peterson was sentenced to death, though the appeals that will be filed will drag things out for years. Elected officials in California and Massachusetts took the law into their own hands and authorized same-sex marriages, bringing the matter into the 2004 election and almost guaranteeing that it will wind up before the U.S. Supreme Court before too long.

The Boston Red Sox proved miracles can still happen as they won the World Series. The Bucs didn't do quite so well, but as any loyal fan knows, there's always next year.

A LOOK BACK AT 2007

W ell, it seems like it was only yesterday that I was trying to remember what happened in 2006 so I could write a column on it. A lot of things seem to have happened only yesterday, a feeling that seems to get worse the older I get.

One thing that has been happening for far too many yesterdays is the 2008 election. The candidates have achieved what I thought was impossible – they have made a political junkie like me sick of the whole thing. And worse, it isn't over yet!

Yeah, things will tone down once people actually get to vote and the contenders start dropping out of the race. We will then get treated to the losers heaping praise on their party's candidate of choice after spending all of this year comparing them to Satan.

One thing that happened in 2007 is I got a lot more cynical about the political process than I used to be. It didn't help that a lot of this year was taken up with a discussion about illegal immigration, with anyone asking that the law be upheld being labeled as racist. It's an unsolved problem, and I'll probably have something to say about it in the end of the year column of 2008.

Meanwhile, we are still in Iraq. The good news is less people are dying. The bad news is it is still a political mess over there. Maybe the losers of the presidential primaries should run over there and give them a hand?

On a more entertaining note, three tales were completed. We learned the fate of The Boy Who Lived as "Harry Potter and the Deathly Hallows" was eagerly greeted by hordes of readers. "Spiderman 3" was greeted with mixed reviews by the Ware household, with me loving it and my sons deriding it as "Peter Parker goes emo." Finally, "Pirates of the Caribbean" finished (at least for the moment) the story of Jack Sparrow, Will Turner, and Elizabeth Swann. Who knew a pirate in eyeliner could be so cool?

OJ Simpson proved that some celebrity crime suspects don't go away, no matter how much you'd like them to. Lindsey Lohan, Britney Spears, and Paris Hilton made me grateful once again that I've never had to try to raise a girl. Anna Nicole Smith demonstrated that almost anything can be made front page news if the press keeps talking about it over and over again.

A troubled student at Virginia Tech killed 32 fellow students and gave parents of college students more reasons to lose sleep. A bridge in Minneapolis collapsed, and we were glued to our television sets as people were rescued by fellow travelers and bystanders.

Gas prices soared to new heights with no signs of dropping. Iran's president Mahmoud Ahmadinejad came to the United States and spoke to Columbia University, exercising the kind of free speech most of his countrymen don't enjoy. The debate on whether or not Iran has nuclear weapons got both more and less clear, with one report saying Iran had quit working on their nuclear program several years ago amid some criticism. North Korea agreed to disable its nuclear weapons, thus making the world a tiny bit safer, at least for now.

Hurricane predictions were proven wrong for the second year in a row, and most Floridians were glad of it. Wildfires raged in California again, which for some reasons surprised some, at least if you watched the news coverage.

So now we're looking at 2008, with more news, more politics, and more oddball stuff to fill columns with. Hopefully, it will go slower – or at least seem to.

A LOOK BACK AT 2008

It seems odd to be writing my end of year column while there's still about a week left to the year. Such is the nature of deadlines.

I have to start this column off with the election of Barack Obama as President of the United States. No, I didn't vote for him. But even I acknowledge that for a country that fifty years ago was still forcing African Americans to drink at separate water fountains this was an historic vote. Will people who are bent on seeing nothing good in this country acknowledge we've made progress in this area? One would hope so.

This was the year conservatives felt left out in the cold by both major political parties. The only bright spot for us was Sarah Palin, who was proven to be a conservative by the way the media savaged her.

I mentioned last year that I thought illegal immigration would still be a big issue in 2008. Given we've heard almost nothing about it this year, I think I've flunked as a psychic.

Another thing I didn't predict was the financial crisis which gave us the spectacle of big businesses marching up to Congress and begging for help, making the word "bailout" the new buzzword of the decade.

Fortunately for a lot of us, gas prices dropped to reasonable levels after climbing up into the stratosphere. There's even talk of gas dropping down to under $1 a gallon in 2009, though cynics like me will only believe it when we see it.

Sadly, we'll probably be hearing the name Illinois Governor Rod Blagojevich a lot in 2009, because even though there's a lot of evidence proving he's not exactly free from corruption, he's decided to try to outlast his accusers. More reasons to be cynical about politics, though this might at least be mildly entertaining.

Two names I hope drop into obscurity in 2009, though I wouldn't bet on it: William Ayers and the Reverend Jeremiah Wright.

Person who offers a compelling argument for karma: OJ Simpson, who will be doing jail time for his badly thought out escapade in Vegas last year. Were the jurors swayed by his acquittal for murder all those years ago? I don't know. And there's a lot of people out there who don't care.

In entertainment news, "The Dark Knight" was a big hit in the Ware household as well as a lot of other places. Heath Ledger's Joker was impressive and award worthy, which makes his premature death all the more tragic.

In other entertainment news, I discovered Stephanie Meyers' *Twilight* series, as did a bunch of movie goers. It's a new and interesting take on the vampire story, and the writer in me wants to rip the books apart to find out how Meyers wove such an engaging tale.

In 2008, we sadly said goodbye to (among others) Charlton Heston, who would forever be the picture of Moses to some; William F. Buckley and Jesse Helms, conservative voices now silenced; Michael Crichton, a great writer who told us of dinosaur DNA and kept us on the edge of our seats with his thrillers; Tony Snow and Tim Russert, who were classy newsmen; and Bobby Fischer, chess prodigy that adulthood was not kind to.

In the Ware household, my oldest son John got engaged to be married (yes, there will be a column about the wedding) and James left the nest as a period of my life ended. A new one now begins. More about that in 2009.

A LOOK BACK AT 2009

A h, it's that time of year again – when I dive into the foggy darkness that is my memory and talk about the high (or low) points of the year.

Of course, as I type this, the year isn't over yet. Deadlines mean that there's more than a week left to 2009. But more than enough stuff has happened this year to fill my space, and if something else big happens there's always next week, right?

But let's look back and the crazy and news-filled year that was...

In January, Barack Obama was inaugurated as President. This event managed to cause brain cells of people at both extremes of the political spectrum to explode, which explains some of the weirder things that were said at times.

After becoming President, Obama managed to speak so well about how badly we need peace that the Nobel committee decided that even though he hadn't done anything to move it along, he deserved the Peace Prize. I will leave it to readers to decide if this was further evidence of brain cells exploding.

By the way, 2009 is ending with US soldiers still in Iraq and Afghanistan. While we may reduce our numbers in Iraq, it looks like we're not leaving the Middle East any time soon.

The economy continued to falter, leading to all kinds of businesses closing and a lot of discussion about what to do about it. Those graduating from college this year, John among them, were warned that this wasn't the greatest job market to break into. Thankfully, John managed and at this point in time is employed, albeit part-time.

Along with the economy, President Obama spent a good part of the year dealing with health care. A Democratic Congress and Senate were more than willing to oblige, despite loud protests from voters during town hall meetings. And to date no one has yet convinced me that the federal government's taking over health care is constitutional.

The economy and health care added fuel to a discontent fire that led to tea parties no longer just meaning scones and cucumber sandwiches, but gatherings of unhappy voters wanting to be heard. The groups were laughed at, dismissed, but are still there, a shadow that we may see covering the 2010 elections.

Sarah Palin published an autobiography that in part jabbed those who made her life so difficult in 2008. Only time will tell if she has any desire for a future in politics.

Star Trek came back, reinvented but still close enough to the original to satisfy Trekkers like myself. This month, "Avatar" opened to huge audiences who loved the incredible visuals.

We discovered with Twitter we could say a lot in 140 characters. Amazon's Kindle let us load a small library of books onto a device lighter than my laptop.

Michael Jackson died with as much attention and controversy as he lived. Ted Kennedy joined his brothers Bobby and John in the next life. Farrah Fawcett, an actress who started out as one of Charlie's Angels, lost a long battle with cancer.

On the personal front, as I mentioned earlier in this column, my oldest son John graduated from college. Thanks to him I also became a mother-in-law to one of the sweetest, kindest young women on the planet, Amanda. Whatever else may have come out of 2009, that alone makes it a good year for me.

May 2010 have good things for us as well.

A LOOK BACK AT 2010

G rab something to hold on to – we're going to take a quick look back at the crazy year that was 2010 right as we dive into 2011.

Where do I start? Perhaps with the mid-term elections, which made it clear that Americans were very ticked off by how things have been going. The tea parties, which got their start in 2009, grew bigger and louder as the year went on, and deserve some credit (or blame) for how things turned out. The upshot is that we will start the new year with a Republican House and a Democratic Senate – and there will be plenty of fireworks before it's all over.

Some of the fireworks will deal with health care reform, which got passed this year. As the months went by and people realized what had been done, the popularity of the bill sank like a lead balloon. Will it survive court challenges and a new Congress? I hope not, but time will tell.

This year we also dealt with a massive oil spill courtesy of BP, whose bosses proved that they badly needed better people skills. It was finally dealt with, but not before we were bombarded with numerous pictures of oil-soaked birds and ongoing video of the stuff spilling out into the ocean.

The economy continues to stutter along, though it has a long way to go. Depending on who you talked to, stimulus bills either helped or hurt things. The government decided at the last minute to extend all of the Bush tax cuts, at least for now. This was greeted with a sigh of relief by a lot of people.

In January Apple introduced the iPad, a huge gizmo that I surprisingly am not lusting after. I have decided I want a Kindle, however, and those who heard me say earlier that I wouldn't get a free "I told you so." Apple still got some of my money this year: while the iPad doesn't appeal to me, I love my iPod Touch.

Speaking of the Kindle, one new thing for me this year is that I've started publishing short stories online. If you have a spare 99 cents and want a quick read, you can see a list of what I've got here: http://www.smashwords.com/profile/view/jjpress.

The biggest news on the anti-terrorism front was how the TSA was getting touchy-feely with flyers. Despite videos and criticism the patdowns continue to go on, and a planned Thanksgiving week protest fizzled.

Our borders are still not secure. People against illegal immigration were labeled as racist and anti-immigration period. Very little progress has been made this year on the subject – maybe we'll have better luck in 2011.

Haiti suffered a devastating earthquake they are still recovering from. Nashville flooded. Many parts of our country is buried in snow, and I'm sure someone is blaming all this on global warming.

We all spent a lot of time on Facebook and Twitter, which raised privacy issues even while more of us tuned in online. Tiger Woods and Mel Gibson both showed us how bad people can be, while the rescue of the Chilean miners gave us a reason to cheer.

On a personal note, John and Amanda moved to Sebring, something good for both me and Highlands County. I wrote 50,000 words during National Novel Writing Month. And I continued to enjoy spending time with you, my readers. We may not always agree, but I value your support and thank you for a great 2010. I hope you'll stay with me as we push forward to 2011.

A LOOK BACK AT 2011

I t's that time of year again – when I take a few moments to look back over the year we've just survived and hit some of the highlights that occurred. Or as many as can fit in the column, anyway.

According to Harold Camping, we aren't meant to be around. He predicted the world was going to end on May 21st, which came and went without incident. He later revised his prediction to October 21st, which also came and went with us still around. Of course, there are those who predict the world is going to end at the conclusion of 2012, so we're not done with the doomsayers yet.

But in my opinion, the big news this year was the economy, which continues to sputter along more or less. During the several "crises" we've endured with the federal budget this year, both Democrats and Republicans proved that when the going gets tough, the tough calls the other side names and hurls accusations. This made for a lot of last-minute deals and bad feelings all around, which tells me this next year will be interesting politically speaking.

Dissatisfaction with the economy and perceived "fat cats" led to the Occupy Wall Street movement, which spread to other cities in the country and had a big impact on the news. It has since faded away from the front pages, and I'm not sure what if anything they managed to accomplish, except some attention.

Protests broke out in various countries of the world, including the Middle East. The results of this "Arab Spring" are still being determined but led to the downfall of President Mubarak of Egypt and Moammar Khadafy of Libya.

Other political news has to do with Republican presidential candidates. Donald Trump made headlines as he flirted with the idea of running, then backed off. He claims he might still run after all, which means he will probably still be on the radar in 2012.

The rest of the Republican field held approximately 2,134 debates, most of which told us nothing new and changed few minds. Favorites came and went, including Herman Cain, who was forced to drop out after being accused of sexual impropriety. Everyone who had anything to bad to say about him fell silent after he left the race, which makes me wonder if that was the whole idea.

The rest of the Republican crowd continue to jockey for position, and while Mitt Romney appears to hold his own there is still a strong "anybody but Romney" vibe in the race. With primaries finally happening, people will finally be able to vote – if the debates didn't burn them out so badly they choose to ignore the whole thing.

Osama Bin Laden was finally caught and killed, closing a door that he opened on 9/11. Steve Jobs passed away, to the sorrow of geeks everywhere. The creator of "The Family Circus," Bil Keane, succumbed to congestive heart failure. Other significant deaths include Christopher Hitchens, Kim Jong-Il, and Andy Rooney.

Earthquakes rocked Japan and the east coast of the United States. Japan's earthquake brought on a tsunami, which added to the disaster. In Highlands County we had our normal weather for the year and were blessed with no hurricanes to trouble us.

In personal news, I've continued to epublish short stories online for readers to download onto their personal ereaders. This month I published my first novel, "Dead Hypocrites." If you enjoy a Christian mystery, please check it out.

A lot more happened in 2011, but I'm just about out of room. There will be a lot happening in 2012, I'm sure. I look forward to writing about it.

A LOOK BACK AT 2012

I t's that time of the year again – time when I take a quick peek back at the year and use this column to hit the highlights that occurred. Of course, these highlights are the things that interest me the most, regardless of whether or not they are all that important.

The big news this year was, of course, was the presidential election. It started with a Republican primary that gave us Mitt Romney versus Anyone Except Mitt Romney. Governor Romney emerged victorious but bloodied and took on President Obama. Two conventions, several debates, and a lot of political ads later, President Obama emerged victorious, ready to take on a second term on the promise that he'll do better. His victory garnered him Time's Person of the Year award, which ticked a few people off. Others got upset over those ticked off, and it seems that our political discourse isn't going to improve in the near future.

Of course, the fiscal cliff has also taken up the news at the moment, which to date has not been resolved by the politicians. There's a chance that by the time you read this they will have come to their senses and hammered something out that will benefit the country. On the other hand, there's also a chance that unicorns are real. So forgive me for not holding my breath on this one.

In other political news, the Supreme Court upheld Obamacare, to the surprise of many like myself who couldn't find "health care" in the Constitution. We are now apparently stuck with Obamacare now, and let's hope it's not as bad as it looks.

Hurricane Sandy paid a visit to the Northeast, garnering the sympathy of many in the South who felt their pain. Here in Highlands County we managed to escape any major weather events, except for the inevitable heat wave this summer that we endure to pay for nice winters.

The end of the world that some claimed the Mayans predicted came and went with northing much happening. It did generate a lot of jokes which people cracked before, during, and after the fizzled apocalypse.

Several mass shootings left us grieving for the lives lost and debating gun control for the umpteenth time. Here in Florida, a neighborhood watch volunteer who is white/Hispanic shot and killed a young black man, claiming Florida's "Stand Your Ground" law. This case will undoubtedly be part of 2013's news, at least here in Florida.

In entertainment news, Disney made plans to buy Lucasfilm, which gave geeks all over the world hopes for more Star Wars movies, as long as Disney was smart and got rid of Jar-Jar Binks.

We finally had to say goodbye to Dick Clark, who had seemed to have the gift of living forever. Writer Ray Bradbury passed away, leaving a wealth of reading for eager bookworms. Robert Bork, whose contentious confirmation hearings for the Supreme Court in 1987 was the start of the process going downhill, also left us. Neil Armstrong, the first man to walk on the moon, embarked on the greatest adventure. Other deaths that caught our attention this year include Whitney Houston, Jack Klugman, Larry Hagman, and Arlen Specter.

Personally, 2012 was a year of ups and downs. I lost two very dear to me, my father-in-law and my beloved beagle. In good news, I continued to write and saw two of my novels go into print and become available via amazon.com. Also, James graduated from college and my nest became a little emptier – I leave it to you if that is a good or bad thing to happen this year.

Other things happened this year, but I'm out of space. We'll just have to push ahead to 2013, where I hope to continue to entertain you and maybe make you think once in a while. Thanks for reading.

A LOOK BACK AT 2013

It's that time of the year again, when I pause a moment to look back over the past 12 months and pick a few news items to highlight over the past year. Not everything, mind you, just those things I feel deserve attention and snarky comments.

Washington, DC gave us plenty of news this year. There was the rollout of Obamacare, which did a rather impressive crash and burn thanks to all the technical glitches. I didn't do a column about the rollout because to do it right I would have had to visit healthcare.gov, and with all the problems it was having I was afraid to. I'm told the site has improved, but given the low numbers of people who've actually been able to get health care through it and concerns about how safe your personal information is on the site, I wouldn't call this a win yet.

Sort of related to Obamacare was the government shutdown, which lasted long enough to make everyone fed up with politics as usual. Republicans tried to defund the health care act and failed, and thus became the whipping boys for the shutdown. And many Congressmen continued to get paid during the time, while furloughed government workers had to dip into savings to keep afloat. There is something very wrong with that picture.

It is little wonder that President Obama and Congress are both suffering from low approval numbers. I would like to think that they would learn from this and do better in 2014, but I am not holding my breath.

On a more positive note, the Duchess of Cambridge had a baby this year, which sent Britons into a wild tizzy of cuteness overload. The baby, whose name is (I am not kidding) His Royal Highness Prince George Alexander Louis of Cambridge, is as cute as anything, but had to wear some weird clothes from time to time. Part of being royal, I guess.

This year saw Pope Benedict step down from being the head of the Catholic church, a move that left non-Catholics like me asking how someone "de-Popes." His replacement, Pope Francis, has been very popular, earning Time's Person of the Year Award and having a reputation of being a "people's Pope." Some conservatives have questioned some of his beliefs, but they are drowned out by a media that is in love. Time will tell how long this honeymoon lasts.

The Boston Marathon was allegedly targeted by two brothers who apparently planted homemade bombs near the finish line. Three people were killed and over 200 wounded. The country was more mad than terrorized by this act, and the Boston Marathon will go on.

Nelson Mandela passed away this year, leaving a large hole in the South African psyche. Tom Clancy and Michael Palmer both went to the great word processor in the sky. Other deaths this year include James Gandolfini, Peter O'Toole, and Joan Fontaine.

As for the Ware household in 2013, Don and I celebrated our 30th wedding anniversary by taking a Norwegian cruise. This past summer we got a new member of the family, a beagle named Barney. At this point (the day after Christmas) I've written over 160,000 words of new fiction this year, which include 8 short stories and a novel. Those numbers do not include the column, which averages 600 words a week. It's a lot of words for 2013.

Here is to another year together with you, dear readers, as we continue to look at the world around us and try to make sense of it. Or at least poke fun. Have a happy and safe New Year!

A LOOK BACK AT 2014

I t's time for my annual peek back into the year we're finishing up with so we can hurry up and get to 2015. Of course, as you read this there is still some year left and something else could happen. But for now, the following is some of the highlights so far in 2014.

For example, this year a lot of people got really scared about Ebola getting into the United States. Ebola is a scary disease that has killed thousands in Africa, and the worry some had was that if just one person had it here it would spread all across the fruited plain and many of us would die.

Well, a handful of people in the United States had Ebola...and most of them recovered. The virus didn't spread from the very limited areas it was in, and the story dropped out of sight. Is anyone still worried?

Also, we had midterm elections, where Democrats (mostly) got tossed out and Republicans (mostly) got tossed in. The Republicans now control both the House and the Senate, and 2015 will tell if I and other cynics will be able to detect a difference in governance.

A new terror group called ISIS reared its ugly head, beheading hostages and sweeping parts of the Middle East, taking territory and slaughtering thousands. They are still going strong as I type and may well be a topic for a look back at 2015.

But it wasn't ISIS that caused Sony Entertainment so much grief over the past few weeks. That would be a group probably working for the North Koreans who hacked into their database and released all kinds of information. They were upset over a movie that Sony was releasing that talked about assassinating North Korea leader Kim Jong Un. Threats against theaters that planned to show the movie caused Sony to first pull the film, though they later changed their mind and released it to be shown at some independent theaters and online. Hooray for free speech, though to be honest I never had an interest in seeing this film (I suspect it is too raunchy for my taste) and have no plans to see it.

Sadly, evidence of the racial problems that still exist in this country were brought out when a white police officer in Ferguson, Missouri shot and killed an unarmed black man. When the officer wasn't indicted for the shooting riots broke out. A case in New York where a black man died when white officers subdued him also caused an outcry.

And as I type this there is a case in Missouri where a white police officer shot and killed a man who pulled a gun on him and people gathered to protest. Two police officers are dead in New York in what has been reported as a retaliation killing for the Ferguson and New York cases. When will this end?

In more positive news, ice bucket challenges spread all over the place and raised over $100 million for ALS research. This challenge involved dumping a bucket of ice water over one's head and sharing the results on social media. I admit I skipped this particular activity, though I know several people who participated.

Robin Williams took his own life, which made the world a little sadder and raised awareness about clinical depression. Joan Rivers unexpectedly passed away. Jay Lake, a writer I knew slightly who was farther along the road of success than I am, lost his battle with cancer.

In personal news, this year my youngest son James eloped with a lovely girl named Ali, giving me another daughter-in-law to love. I sold a short story to an anthology and published a novel and some short stories. All in all it was mostly a quiet year in the Ware household, with nothing much to report.

A happy New Year to all my readers, and may 2015 bring us all lots of fun things to talk about. I'll be here; I hope you are too.

A LOOK BACK AT 2015

I t's time for my look back at the previous year, when I pick out the events we all chatted about and the "big" news stories of 2015 and cram it all into a column.

This is challenging. A lot happened this year. I have to pick and choose between stories and events. What makes this story more compelling than that one? Why does this one make the cut and the other one gets ignored?

Because I said so, that's why. It's my column and I'm going to focus on those things that caught my particular attention. If I miss something that caught yours, I apologize.

It would be easy to fill this column with Donald Trump news, since he's dominated the political scene since he decided to run last year. He joined countless other Republicans in a quest to become the party's nominee for President and dealt with his critics in a polite and thoughtful manner.

You thought I was serious, didn't you? In reality Trump hasn't met a critic he couldn't denounce and has succeeded in insulting a vast majority of the planet. Somehow this appears to make him popular with people who take polls, but we'll see what happens when actual voting starts.

This year also saw a lot of violence, with episodes of questionable shootings by police officers and armed idiots who brought death and grief to innocents. And in every case reasoned debate was ignored in favor of name calling, posturing, and in some cases, riots.

Last year we were told "black lives matter," a sentiment I share. White, brown, and any other color you can think of lives matter as well. None of this should have to be said, but in 2015 some people felt it bore repeating.

War-torn Syria produced a number of fleeing refugees, and the question of what to do with them became a hot political topic. Compassion warred against caution, and it is a fight I fear will continue into 2016.

Here in Sebring we had an honest to goodness bomb scare, with someone planting a pipe bomb at Newsom Eye Clinic. A suspect was quickly found and arrested, but it was an exciting day for our small town.

Leonard Nimoy, who would always be known for playing Mr. Spock in Star Trek, was beamed up for the last time. Other notable deaths include Mario Cuomo, Meadowlark Lemon, and B. B. King.

But it wasn't all bad news in 2015. Star Wars fans were rewarded for their patience over the past years with "The Force Awakens," a great movie that I've already seen twice and will probably see again at some point.

We received awesome pictures of Pluto, thanks to the New Horizons spacecraft, which gave us a good look at this planet (I know some people think it shouldn't be a planet. These people are wrong).

In personal news I sold three short stories and published a new novel. Two additional dogs came to live with us, and the Ware household remains one of love and barely controlled chaos.

My hope is that 2016 will be a year filled with writing and publishing. And maybe getting my office straightened up. Hey, it could happen.

Whatever you are aiming for in 2016 I hope the year is filled with good things for you. And that you'll keep reading. As long as I can, I aim to keep writing. Here's to a happy new year to us all.

A LOOK BACK AT 2016

The year 2016 is just about over, and for some it cannot end soon enough. Let's face it, this has been a tough year for so many people.

The big news for us in the United States was, of course, the presidential election. Donald Trump beat the odds and the pundits, surprising everyone (including, I suspect, himself) by actually winning the thing. This despite saying things that would've doomed any other candidate to oblivion.

Part of it was that Hillary Clinton simply didn't run that great of a campaign. Yes, I know, there were the email leaks and she kept getting hammered on things like her private email server and Benghazi, but she might have been able to pull it off still if she'd given people a reason to vote for her besides that she wasn't Trump and not ignored certain voting blocs.

That is all in the past, though. We now can look forward to four years of Donald Trump at the helm of the ship of state and pray he doesn't run us into an iceberg. I am sure this column will not be my last mention of him.

In other news, Britons voted to leave the European Union, causing some chaos while everyone tries to sort that out. It turns out one doesn't simply walk away from such a thing, and terms are being thrashed out as I type. It will probably be years before the dust settles on that one, and that's assuming Great Britain doesn't come back with, "We were just kidding."

Then there have been the celebrity deaths of 2016. A lot of talent has left this life. Alan Rickman, who brought Professor Snape to life in the Harry Potter series, left way too early. So did Carrie Fisher, the multi-talented woman who breathed life into Princess Leia. Tragically, her mother Debbie Reynolds followed her in death just one day later.

And that's not even mentioning other notable folk, such as Garry Shandling, David Bowie, and Harper Lee. History will also record that Supreme Court Justice Antonin Scalia and Fidel Castro also passed away this year, making headlines and shaking up the political world some.

Tragedy struck an Orlando nightclub in the worst mass shooting in modern U. S. history. A man who pledged allegiance to the Islamic State shot and killed 49 innocents before dying in a shootout with authorities. Sadly, other terror attacks occurred around the world, and I fear we will see more in 2017.

But there were some bright spots in 2016. The Chicago Cubs took the World Series. People got outdoors and walking while searching for elusive Pokémon. Rio hosted the Olympics.

It would be easy to end this column on a sour note. After all, it's been a tough year. But as I sit here I'm trying to look for the good that happened and could still happen in 2017.

So, here's the good from my perspective. I sold some stuff in 2016. I am on track to finish the first draft of a novel before the year is over. Both my sons are healthy and happy.

This next year I will celebrate my 34th year married to Don, who has been a great support and blessing this past year. He refuses to let me quit, and even lets me talk about him here.

The column is still a thing, and I look forward to sharing things that interest me with you as we journey through the new year. Let's hope and pray for a good one.

A LOOK BACK AT 2017

Because I want to start this column off on a positive note, let me reiterate something I mentioned in passing in an earlier column: in 2018, I will become a grandma for the first time.

To say I am excited about this is an understatement. It is by far the best news I had this year. The baby is due April 3rd, though my son, with his warped sense of humor, is hoping for April 1st.

I am holding on to that bit of good news as I type this column, because to be honest, 2017 was not a year brimming with good things for a lot of people. In fact, I think the majority of Americans will look at this past year and cry "Good riddance!" when the ball drops in Times Square on Sunday.

Let's take the big thing first. Donald Trump was inaugurated as President in January. People from both sides of the political divide decided to lay aside their differences and work together for the sake of the country.

I am kidding about that last, of course. Sadly, the end of the year sees us more divided than the beginning. And instead of having a conversation with those they don't agree with, way too many people would rather be insulting or dismissive of those on the other side. It doesn't look to improve in 2018, though I will point out if you aren't trying to communicate and work with your political opponent, you are part of the problem, not the solution.

There was also a horrifying number of women coming out with accusations of sexual assault or harassment. I say horrifying because men should be living in such a righteous way that there shouldn't be one woman feeling she was harmed in this way. Men in politics, news, and entertainment were called out on their behavior. My hope is that the light brought to bear on this awful behavior will mean that people will know better than to act this way to others.

Several powerful hurricanes paid the US a visit. The one that stands out for me is Irma, because she slammed into the county I live in and did us a lot of harm. I still see blue tarps on some roofs months later, and I've heard that some families still have badly damaged homes. Not to mention the nightmare in Puerto Rico, which got hit with Irma AND Maria, and is still trying to recover.

We had a number of well-known people say goodbye to us this year. Country music singer Glen Campbell laid his guitar down. Jerry Lewis, the zany comedian who hosted the telethon for muscular dystrophy for ages, also passed away. Della Reese, the actress who will always be the angel Tess from "Touched by an Angel" to me, left us. Others who died this year include Mary Tyler Moore, Gregg Allman, and Chuck Berry.

In personal news this year left me tired and not a little frustrated. The national news was often enough by itself to drive me bonkers, but life in general was not as smooth as I would have liked. While I happily saw some things published this year I didn't write as many words as I would've liked. I'm hoping that will be different in 2018.

My hope and prayer is that 2018 is a better year for all of us. Let's lay down the baggage of 2017 and move on. And together, we can shout "Good riddance!" at midnight on Sunday.

A LOOK BACK AT 2018

I t's almost the end of the year, which means I treat you all to a column where I look back over 2018 and reflect on what high (and low) points occurred that I can fit into 600 words.

The most important thing that happened is obviously the birth of my first grandchild, Lavinia Joanne Ware (you may think something more important happened this year. You would be wrong). Lavinia is a sweet girl who captured my heart before she was born. Watching her grow over these months has been a treat. I'm so grateful to her parents who try to make sure we're a part of her life.

But, yes, I have to admit that there were other things that happened in 2018. So, instead of continuing to tell you about my wonderful granddaughter I will touch on of few of those.

Weatherwise, Highlands County managed to avoid a repeat of 2017, when Irma wreaked havoc upon us. The Florida panhandle wasn't so lucky. Hurricane Michael slammed into those in the panhandle with devastating force. Here's hoping they recover quickly.

Donald Trump remained president, something not everyone is happy about. As I type this a fierce disagreement about a border wall has partially shut down the government, which has put people out of work during the holiday season. Neither Trump nor the Democrats appear likely to budge and break the deadlock, which means that 2019 will be an interesting year. Throw in that the Democrats have retaken the House of Representatives and I think we're all resigned to more political drama.

The #metoo movement was a thing, as women told tales of harassment and abuse and men were brought down by their bad behavior. The movement played a role in Judge Brett Kavanaugh's hearings to become a Supreme Court Justice when a woman accused him of sexual assault. The accusation lacked evidence to back it up, and Kavanaugh succeeded in joining the court, but even now people are divided on what the truth is.

"Divided" would be a good word for 2018. Politics has always been somewhat divisive, but this year more than ever lines were drawn and friendships and family relationships were sundered simply because people didn't agree on something. There was a time we could agree to disagree and remain friends even if we didn't share political views. More and more that is no longer true.

Sadly, there were more mass shootings in 2018. Everyone agrees it's a problem, but no one can agree on a solution. See above about being divided to understand why we can't seem to come up with a way to cut down on these tragedies.

Immigration remained a big issue in 2018. Earlier this year Trump enacted an existing policy to separate children at the Mexican border from their parents trying to gain entry into the US. After a huge outcry, the policy was rescinded, but there is still huge fallout from it. Opinions on our immigration mess range from calling for open borders to shutting the border down altogether. Hopefully, we'll do something positive about this next year, though I'm not holding my breath.

In notable deaths, the lovely Barbara Bush passed away in April, and her husband President George H. W. Bush followed her months later. Stan Lee, superhero creator of Marvel, went to that big comic book shop in the sky. William Goldman, who gave us the iconic "The Princess Bride," passed away, leaving many fans gasping "Inconceivable!" Other notable deaths include Billy Graham, Penny Marshall, and John McCain.

As for me, I celebrated 20 years of "Laura's Look" and got some writing done. Hoping for a more productive 2019 and looking forward to the journey. Thanks for coming with me.

A LOOK BACK AT 2019

I t's that time of year again, when I look back at the previous year and try to hit the highlights in about 600 words.

Normally I save personal stuff for the end of the column, but with three profound events taking place this year I feel the need to mention them first.

First, this year we said goodbye to my beloved mother-in-law, who passed away at the age of 91. Yesterday was Christmas, and I felt the loss keenly. While we had a good day, there was an undercurrent of sadness that she wasn't there to share it with us.

The same day we lost Mom, we also lost Barney, the old beagle we adopted in 2013. Barney's antics occasionally graced this space. While he lived a good long life and sometimes got on the naughty dogs list, he was still loved, and his passing hit me hard.

On a positive note, we welcomed Matthias Raymond Ware last week, the son of my oldest son John and his wife Amanda. I'm not sure what big sister Lavinia thinks of this development, but I think she's going to love him. I know I do and can't wait to see him and kiss those plump cheeks.

Unfortunately, 2019 hasn't been the best year for our country. And despite my attempts to be positive, there are things that occurred this year I can't ignore. So, take a deep breath as we go on...

In January of this year, Sebring joined the ranks of communities that suffered mass shootings. Someone murdered five women at a local bank, and then surrendered to authorities. I'm not sure how this will play out in the courts. But it had a profound effect on my county, that is still felt almost a year later.

Nationally, the big news is that President Donald Trump was impeached by the House of Representatives. There is a lot of political posturing going on with this from both sides, and a trial, if there is one (yes, there is question about that) will be held next year and is guaranteed to be a circus. The whole thing is a symptom of a huge problem in our country, which I plan to address in a future column.

Also, we had what sometimes felt like thousands of Democrats running for President. Some of that crowd have dropped out, but there's still enough players you need a program to sort them all out. Next year is going to be bruising as a nominee comes out and we battle through a presidential election. While I'm a political junkie, I find myself apprehensive for the coming year.

In movies, Star Wars ended their saga with "The Rise of Skywalker," which, depending on who you talk to, is a great coda to the franchise or a train wreck. For what it's worth, I liked it enough to watch it twice, and lean more towards a positive review than a negative one.

Of course, other stuff happened this year. There were notable deaths and incidents, but as I pointed out in the beginning of this column, I only have around 600 words to recount them all. My hope for you, my readers, is that more good things than bad happened to you this year, and that 2020 will be filled with blessings.

And, to end on a positive quote, I give you the words of my youngest son James, who helpfully gave me the ending line to this column: "We are still here."

A LOOK BACK AT 2020

If you're reading this column the day after Christmas, you might be asking yourself, "Self, why is Laura doing her year end column now, when there's almost a week left to the year?"

Fair question. It comes down to tradition. My year end column usually appears on the last Saturday of the year. I admit this year it's a risky proposition, given that 2020 has taught us anything can and just might happen. But I have plenty to talk about even without the extra week thrown in. Say what you must, 2020 wasn't exactly a dull year.

To start with, there's the pandemic, which we all hoped would go away quickly when it reared its ugly head back in March. Here it is December and we're still dealing with the effects COVID-19 has wreaked on us. There are businesses that will never recover because they were forced to close to slow the spread of the virus. Many, if not most of us, wear masks when dealing with the outside world, and a lot of us have embraced Zoom meetings and other technology that helped us keep in touch with each other.

There is a light at the end of the tunnel. Two vaccines have been FDA approved, and as I speak are being distributed throughout our nation. It's possible this thing will be in our rear view mirror by this time next year, if not sooner. Nevertheless, it has changed us in many ways, not all of them for the better.

Then there's a contentious presidential election that made 2000 seem like child's play. This time Florida was not the target of election ire, in fact, we were praised for getting it right. But several states came up with issues, some real, some imagined, and even as I type this two days before Christmas there are those who doubt the results.

The election – in fact, the year – displayed us at our worst: divided, sniping, tossing accusations like firebombs into the debate. I worry about the division because I know how badly it weakens us as a nation. Some say it's always been there. But I can still remember a time when people could debate with respect for each other and even work together despite their differences. Those days almost seem gone forever.

Our divisions were also on display as some questionable actions by a few policemen against African Americans lit the fuse on a powder keg that saw people take to the streets in protest. It seemed impossible to say anything without being accused of saying it wrong, so some chose silence, and were condemned for even that.

And, thanks to COVID-19 and just the passage of time, we lost many who were mourned. I normally cite a few deaths of famous people at this point. But in 2020 it seems right to just point out that as of today, over 300,000 Americans have died from the coronavirus, and the number worldwide is 1.72 million.

There IS one thing almost everyone can agree on – 2020 was not a year filled with fond memories. But even in the darkest times, there are pinpoints of light.

I met my grandson, Matthias, in 2020, though he was born at the end of 2019. I have been able to watch him and his older sister grow thanks to a few visits to them and the magic of technology. These two bring me joy even in the midst of a pandemic.

And Marie, a kind reader of this column, sent me a gift of dark chocolate. That and your note was a day brightener. Thank you so much.

And thank all of you who read this column of mine and enjoy it. May 2021 be the bringer of better things for all of us.

A LOOK BACK AT 2021

Y'all remember back in 2020, when we looked forward to 2021? We figured things were going to get better and we'd be well on the road to normalcy. Right?

Well, THAT didn't work out as planned...

The first clue that 2021 was going to have issues hit on January 6th, when people who'd swallowed the lies that Joe Biden had somehow stolen the presidential election stormed the Capitol building, hunting for elected officials. Someone went as far as to string up a noose, and chaos ensued.

I realize some readers don't like Joe Biden. I'm not crazy about the job he's been doing as president. But this was wrong on so many levels. And it makes me angry that some people insist on downplaying it as not a big deal. If Democrats had behaved in this fashion, those same people would be shouting for blood.

That began a year that was filled with issues. COVID continued to be a big part of our lives as several variants came on the scene. Some people got vaccinated; others refused, ignoring sound medical advice in the name of "their rights."

I'd like to believe that COVID will be less of an issue in 2022. I am not hopeful.

The economy isn't doing as well as anyone would like it to be. Labor continues to be in short supply for a number of reasons. Supply chain "issues" means things aren't being delivered in a timely fashion. Prices on all kinds of things have shot up. And our leaders are too busy pointing fingers at each other to actually deal with it.

Sadly, we are still very divided as a nation. Instead of pulling together to get out of the mess we're in, we're set up in our own little camps and not even talking to each other. I fear people are withdrawing into what I call "echo chambers:" only surrounding themselves with people who agree with them and not even trying to listen to the other side.

There were a number of notable deaths in 2021. The one that had the most impact on me was the death of my father, who passed away unexpectedly in May. Losing him made a tough year that much more difficult to bear. Thankfully, I have people who care about me and continue to be a support.

All was not grim in 2021. I got to spend time with the grandbabies – in fact, I will start 2022 traveling to South Carolina, where I will assist my son John in the care and feeding of those precious children while their mom is out of town. It is something I'm looking forward to.

And then there's the writing. Readers of this column know I passed three hundred thousand words for the year recently. That is not the only writing milestone I hit.

At the beginning of 2021, I committed to writing a short story a week for a year – 52 short stories. It wasn't always easy – I sometimes got awfully close to the deadline. There were late nights and dealing with writer's block and life trying to get in the way.

This past Sunday I turned in story number 52 and completed my goal. I now have fifty-two additional short stories to send to magazines or publish myself. I will probably do some of both.

In 2022 I am going to drop the pace a bit to go back to some novels I neglected in 2021. And I plan to get a lot more stuff out for people to read. Hopefully, that's a good thing.

I am grateful for my readers, who have endured 2021 with me. Let's hope and pray 2022 is a better year for us. We need it to be.

A LOOK BACK AT 2022

Reading over a column I wrote around a year ago titled, "A Look Back at 2021," I see that I expressed the hope that 2022 would turn out to be a better year for us. As I regard how it actually turned out, I would say it was a mixed bag.

COVID, for example, was still a thing in 2022 – but we finally seemed to make some peace with it. It's still out there, and you still don't want to catch it – I say this as one who came down with it in July of this year – but it's less an emergency and more a part of what we deal with from day to day.

Except in China, which has seen protests over their restrictive COVID policies. Apparently, cases have soared in that country and the government is attempting to crack down.

In February of this year, Russia invaded Ukraine in an attempt to seize the country for their own. The Russians supposedly thought this would be quick and effective. Thanks in no small part to help from the West and the Ukrainians' unwillingness to lay down and take it, we're at the end of the year and while Russia has managed to grab parts of the country's east and south, they've failed to achieve the victory they wanted.

Will the Russians give up in 2023? Putin is crazy enough to keep pushing. I think it's a lost cause for him, but he can't bear to admit that. Maybe someone in the government will talk sense to him. Or replace him. We shall see.

In the United States we had midterm elections that surprised a lot of people, me included. We were led to believe there would be a "red wave" of Republicans sweeping House and Senate races and getting majorities in both. Instead, it was a trickle, and while Republicans narrowly did gain control of the House, the Senate is firmly in the hands of Democrats.

I'm not expecting a lot to get done in Congress this year. They will be too busy investigating each other and behaving like spoiled two-year-olds.

Roe v. Wade, the 1973 Supreme Court decision that granted the right to get an abortion, was overturned, to the people's joy or outrage depending on who you were. It put a spotlight on the court and made people wonder if it was time to term-limit judges. I suspect this debate to continue all the way to 2024, so stay tuned.

In Britain, Queen Elizabeth, who'd been queen longer than I've been alive, passed away. King Charles III now reigns and the drama with his family continues. I don't know enough about the man to say if he will do a good job or not, but I do wish him well.

Inflation soared in the US and throughout the world. We continued to struggle with supply chain issues. Crypto currency tanked badly (don't feel badly if you don't understand it, I don't either). Elon Musk got his hands on Twitter, and it is such a mess at the moment I'm glad I have a minimal presence in it.

Personally, this year went okay for the Ware household. I continued to write something every day, passing the 900-day mark on December 15th. I managed to get a couple of things published and while I'd have liked to do more, I'm grateful for what I managed.

I'm hoping for a more productive 2023. And if I'm lucky, you will continue to make the journey with me. Thanks for reading and encouraging this crazy columnist. I hope your 2023 is blessed.

RIPPED FROM THE HEADLINES

These columns were based on news stories, some bigger news than others. Looking at them, I was surprised at how much of the news I cited was negative. But that seems to be the way of big news – it's very rarely about something positive.

There is at least one exception to this. "Forgive This Much" is about something bad that happened, but the focus is on the good that sprouted out from it. It's a column I felt deserved a place in this collection.

A NEW DAY OF INFAMY

September 11th, 2001. My day had begun like a normal day - get up, get the kids off to school, fix a cup of coffee, turn on the radio. I also read the chapter my Ladies Bible Class would be discussing and like the nerdette I am, checked my email.

While I was doing this, the 9:00 AM news came on. And that is when I heard the beginning. A plane had crashed into the World Trade Center building.

At first, I thought it might be a tragic accident of some kind. Then it became clear that not one, but TWO planes had hit the towers in New York. One is an accident; two can't be. I left the radio and switched on the TV. While I watched, they replayed the footage of the second plane striking the building. I felt sick.

I tried to reach a friend of mine who lived in nearby New Jersey to be sure she had not been in the area. I got her answering machine. I asked her to email me and let me know she was OK. Then, I got into my car and drove to church for our Ladies Bible Study.

When I got there, other women were talking about what happened. Then our preacher came in and told us the latest; the Pentagon had been hit by an airplane. We were shocked. As more women arrived, we told them the news and asked if they had heard anything more.

We always open our class with a prayer. That morning, several prayers were offered. For our nation. For our leaders. For those who might be trapped in the buildings. For the families of the dead.

The hour was odd. Two or three times the phone in the secretary's office rang, and since our preacher had left I would slip out of class and answer it. Almost every call had more bad news. A plane was down in Pittsburgh. The towers of the World Trade Center had collapsed. It was horrible to hear.

After class, an older lady I respect took me by the shoulders. "You must be calm now," she instructed me, "for the sake of your boys." I was thankful for her words because I knew she was right. My children would take a cue from my reaction; this was not the time for panic.

I stopped quickly at the store to pick up milk. While there, my cell phone rang; one of my sisters, checking in with me. None of my family live in any of the affected areas. Still, there was a need to touch base with each other, to hear voices, to assure ourselves we were OK.

Once I got home, I fired up my phone and email. I have several friends over the Internet that I communicate with - I went about trying to get in touch with people I knew lived in some of the areas that had been attacked, and I wanted to be sure they were OK. My Star Trek message boards were filled with similar inquiries. "I don't care where you live, post something so we'll know you're okay," pleaded one message. Happily for me, all the people I knew turned out to be fine, though not without losses in their lives.

Then the boys came home. John was angry but contained. James was just angry. He wanted us to go after whoever had done this. He had seen some of the footage on television at school; it had struck him at the very core of his being.

As I look at this, as I get more and more information, as the death toll rises, I find myself experiencing shock mixed with anger. How dare someone do this to my country? How dare they use helpless Americans to make whatever point they feel was important to make?

And how dare they do it behind a curtain - they were ashamed enough of their actions to hide, but not ashamed enough to stop. I was not born when Pearl Harbor occurred. Now I begin to understand the national rage that gripped us then and is sweeping over us now.

We will find them. Whatever our flaws, there is this quality about us - like a large family, we may shout and scream at each other, we may argue politics til the cows come home, but let someone mess with us, we will lay aside our differences and make sure they regret it. We will do what it takes to make sure they will never harm others the way they harmed us.

We have been told to live as normally as we can in light of this. I have tried today. I took the kids to school. I worked in the church office. I kept a doctor appointment. I went to church this evening. I am typing this column. But this national tragedy casts a long, dark shadow over everything.

At one point yesterday, James said to me, "Mom, the worst thing is I will always remember this. And I don't want to."

I know what you mean, honey. I know what you mean.

MAKING HAY ON 9/11

I would like to be able to say that most people have been aboveboard, sensitive, and without fault concerning the incidents surrounding 9/11. That no one had tried to use the tragedy to promote their own interests and futures or line their pockets.

I would also like to be able to say that a hot fudge sundae a day is recommended for a good diet, but that would be lying too.

Unfortunately, there are human beings on the planet that have all the sensitivity and caring of a water buffalo with a migraine. These people look at incidents like the terror attacks and the cash registers that are where their hearts ought to be start ringing. They don't give one thought of how others might feel about their acts.

For example: two days after the Twin Towers collapsed I heard from a friend that some people had taken rubble from the towers to auction off on eBay. The online auction company, according to the story, wisely shut them down. Now, I have not been able to confirm this, so the incident may fall into the category of "urban legend." But, sadly, it's one of those things I could believe happened.

Unfortunately, what I am about to tell you is really going on. CBS is developing a story called "The Real Story of Flight 93," to be told from the perspective of those on the ground. Those involved in it feel it is too early to tell it from the perspective of those on the plane. Now if they could just wise up and realize it's way too soon to tell the story as a movie of the week from any perspective.

CBS already plans to air a two-hour special next month that will contain exclusive video shot during 9/11 in the twin towers after the planes hit. CBS president Leslie Moonves calls the footage moving, vivid, and heroic, and, in the president's opinion, "it was very important as a broadcaster to show this footage."

Important. Yes, I'm sure that's all the motivation involved here. Ratings are the farthest thing from their little brains. It's just a coincidence it's being aired just before the six-month anniversary of the tragedy.

But wait - there's more. A legal battle related to 9/11 is brewing over what is coming out as the most memorable catch phrase of the tragedy; "Let's roll," the last known words of Todd Beamer, one of the passengers on Flight 93 who confronted the hijackers of the plane. A foundation that was set up in Beamer's name wants to trademark the phrase so that any money made from it goes to the victims' families. There are around a dozen other individuals and companies who want the same thing, and at least 2 of them applied for the trademark before the foundation did. "...it's first in, first swim...(I)t's all about good old American capitalism," one of them explained. Capitalism aside, there's a good chance no one will win this one. It's difficult to get trademark protection for common phrases, and certainly "let's roll" was part of the language long before September 11th.

I find myself saddened by all this. It seems those intent on all these projects are forgetting that there were real live people involved in these events. Real people lost husbands and wives and parents and siblings. Real people could see this promoting of those events in the name of capitalism as offensive.

Will that stop any one of these groups from their pursuits? Probably not. After all, this is America, where we pump out all kinds of drivel and call it entertainment. Where we can ignore the grief and feelings of victims and milk a situation for as many dollars as we can pocket. Where we shove microphones into weeping people's faces to ask how they feel about a tragedy and when criticized for it proclaim we are only upholding "The people's right to know."

Perhaps the fact we can do so with the events of 9/11 means we are getting back to normal. Somehow, I cannot rejoice at our "progress."

A YEAR AFTER 9/11

I was rescheduling a doctor's appointment. The receptionist took a moment to check dates and times, and then said, "How about September 11?"

"Oh, wow, what a date," I said wryly.

The lady on the other end of the phone offered to give me another day; apparently several patients had expressed an aversion to coming in that particular day.

"No, that's OK," I said.

September 11. It has been nearly a year since we were riveted to our radios and televisions, watching the terrifying story play out before us. A year since we saw terrorism up close and personal.

As we approach the first anniversary to 9/11, I ask myself what, if anything, has changed. In some ways, things are very much the same. Bin Laden is still being sought by our military. Congress is still acting like sniping is a legitimate form of communication. Polls show that after a brief trip up, American's religious faith is about the same as it was before. For most people, life is going on pretty much as it did before that day.

However, the events of September 11th is not far from our minds. At least, they're not far from my mind, and there must be a lot of people like me out there, because the media is busy feeding us. There are books galore exploring that fateful day. As I type this, a week before the anniversary, I recall a show I watched on the History Channel a day or two ago about the World Trade Center and the items that were found it the rubble. Exploitive? Perhaps. But I will admit I watch them anyway.

Even with the media reminding us of that day, even taking into account you can still see "United We Stand" signs in various windows, and the flags that still wave, the America we live in today is nearly unchanged from the America of a year ago.

One of the problems I've had with writing this column is I'm having trouble deciding if that's a good thing or not.

Some would say that being unchanged is the best revenge against the terrorists. To live our lives the way we've always lived them demonstrates that we are not cowed. There is an argument to be made for this way of thinking. I have even adopted it to a certain extent. I have flown on airplanes this past year. I would add "fearlessly," except that I am never without some trepidation on one of those things - probably because I don't understand how a big heavy airplane can keep itself up in the air in the first place. But I will fly when it is necessary to get to someplace. I would even fly to New York or Washington DC if I could figure out how to pay for it. In this sense, not changing is almost an act of defiance, of saying, "so there!" to the terrorists who would prefer I cower in fear somewhere.

But there is another sense in which we haven't changed, which to me is to our hurt. We have gone back to our old ways of thinking. Some who had filled churches in the days after the tragedy stopped after a while. It's almost as if they'd used God as a spiritual Band-Aid, a quick fix that was discarded as soon as they felt better. As a Christian, I find that sad.

And it didn't take long for politics as usual to crop up either. For approximately three weeks, a breathtaking bipartisanship took hold in the nation's capital. Of course, it didn't last. So once again we have politicians jockeying for power instead of trying to work together. You would think a common threat would have held us together longer.

Let me close out by saying there is one other thing that hasn't changed since 9/11. The Red Cross is in need of blood donations. I took some time this week to make a donation. Why don't you? Give them a call at 382-4499 for their hours of operation and make plans to donate. This is one change we can all agree would be good.

A LOOK AT THE 2002 ELECTIONS

Ok, grab a cup of coffee, pull up a chair, and let's review what happened this week. Hopefully, you voted. If not, well, you're stuck with the results like the rest of us.

First, let me point out that whether you agree with them or not, the Democratic Party miscalculated badly this year. They thought the economy would help them win. They were wrong. They figured they would unseat the President's brother, paying him back for the 2000 election. They failed. They hoped to keep the Senate out of Republican hands. It looks like the Republicans are going to run things for a bit. What happened? My opinion is that the Democratic Party had a bad bout of cluelessness this year, epitomized by Senator Wellstone's funeral-cum-pep rally. I could have told them that would have gone over like a lead brick - my KIDS could have told them that - but somehow they didn't think people would be offended by such a breach of etiquette. Will they learn from this year? Time will tell, but experience has taught me that politicians are not always the best students.

However, I did notice that the media had learned a thing or two. I don't know how many times last night I heard a commentator say, "So and so is ahead, but we're not calling it yet!" If only such restraint had been evident two years ago, maybe I would have gotten more sleep that fall.

And I am proud of the fact that turnout was up this time. Over 50% of Highlands County turned out, to my pleasant surprise. Of course, being the demanding political junkie that I am, I am hoping this will be even higher next time around. (By the way, if this was NOT higher than normal, please don't tell me. I'd rather cling to my illusions).

However, I have to admit that my feelings concerning the votes on the ballot initiatives were less than thrilled. I was especially irritated by the passage of what I have come to think of as "the pregnant pigs amendment." Come on, everyone, last time I looked, the Florida Constitution was for PEOPLE, not animals. If my dog ever finds out about this, he'll petition for a constitutional amendment giving him the right to eat at the table and raid the garbage to his heart's content.

Then there's the tourist tax. I suppose the fact it passed this time around lends credence to the saying, "if at first you don't succeed, try, try, again." All right, it's passed. Good job. Now you need to convince people like me who opposed the thing that you were correct.

Since it is obvious that, under the right circumstances, Floridians will put ANYTHING on the ballot , I want to close out this column with a list of Constitutional amendments I would like to see passed in the future:

Radio talk show hosts who make fun of chocolate lovers shall be fined two hot fudge sundaes per offense, to be paid to the Secretary of Chocolate, who would be me.

People who get into the "10 items or less" checkout line with more than ten items shall be forced to purchase and eat one pound of Brussels sprouts per offense. This will not only get a lot of these people out of the line, it will do wonders for the Brussels sprout industry.

Drive-thru windows that mess up your order should be required to give you a free meal. If they mess up your child's order, the manager is required to babysit the child one hour per mistake.

No parent shall be required to cook more than one meal per mealtime. Family members who don't like what is offered will have the Constitutional right to one of three choices; 1) eat it anyway, 2) fix yourself something (but you have to wash ALL the dishes), or 3) take the cook out to dinner. Making disparaging remarks about the cook's choices voids all the above rights.

If you think of any Constitutional amendments you'd like to see, send them to me. If I get enough of them, I'll put them in a column. Remember, this is the Florida Constitution. If you can dream it, we can get it on the ballot!

A NON-FAN'S VIEW OF DEFLATE GATE

I would not in anyone's mind be considered a football fan. The closest I come to liking football is rooting for the Tampa Bay Buccaneers, which I do because I used to know a player on the team. Because more often than not the Bucs implode, my interest in the football season tends to wane quickly.

I'm barely aware of the fact that the Super Bowl is being played Sunday. I had to look up on Google who was playing (it's the New England Patriots vs. the Seattle Seahawks, for those of you as clueless as I am). I doubt I'll even check in on the game for the commercials – I can always look them up on the Internet on Monday.

But even this non-fan became aware of the latest controversy surrounding the game. I'm speaking of what is being referred to as "Deflate Gate." And as public as that has been, I've still had to do some quick research in order to explain the controversy properly.

So, here is the situation as I understand it (after reading articles on cnn.com, espn.go.com and Wikipedia): During the AFC Championship game between the New England Patriots and the Indianapolis Colts, it was discovered that 11 out of the 12 balls the Patriots were using were underinflated; that is, didn't have as much air as regulations called for.

Why does this matter? According to my research, an underinflated ball is easier to grip, throw, and catch. So if you could get away with it, not fully inflating a ball might give you an advantage in a game.

As I type this, the investigation appears to be ongoing. Patriots' Head Coach Bill Belichick has denied involvement. Quarterback Tom Brady has dismissed the accusations, though he is on record saying he prefers balls that are "deflated."

If it's found to be deliberate, the worst the Patriots face is a hefty fine and maybe losing something called a "draft pick." The game's results will stand (and the deflated balls probably didn't affect the result, according to my research).

So I've just written several hundred words explaining this. Here's the big question I have about it all: So?

People have paid immense attention to this story. In other news, Saudi Arabia's king passed away and Yemen is going through a coup. Those items were barely a blip on the news horizon.

But after spending time looking at this, I wonder what the big deal is. My first thought when I first heard of this was that it might threaten the Patriots' place in the Super Bowl, but that apparently isn't the case. In fact, the likely penalties will amount to a slap on the wrist.

It wasn't that slow of a news week, either. How did this story get to such a level that even non-fans like yours truly got aware of it?

It might be that Americans have weird priorities. Football is important to a lot of my fellow citizens. This might be just the thing to get them excited and worked up. Turmoil in a country they barely know exists? Not so much.

If only people could get as worked up over the state of the country, or the national debt, or even a county commission meeting as they do over a game...

That loud sigh you heard was not a deflating football. That was me.

A COLUMN I DON'T WANT TO WRITE

There is a picture making the rounds on Facebook of a young child. He is clearly having a tantrum while his mom is trying to drag him someplace. The caption goes something like this: "But I don't wanna go vote! I don't like any of these people!"

That meme pretty much sums up my feelings at the moment.

In case you've been off the planet this week, Donald Trump has, for all practical purposes, become the Republican Party's nominee for president (that hurt to type). After being roundly trounced in Indiana, both Ted Cruz and John Kasich chose to leave the race, leaving no one to oppose Trump.

On the Democrat Party side, barring some sort of last-minute miracle, Hillary Clinton will be the nominee. Bernie Sanders has dug in his heels and is determined to go all the way to the convention, but the numbers don't look good for him.

So if you want to look at the two main parties, your choice this November will be between Trump and Clinton. If you are like me, just considering that makes your stomach twist.

How did we get into the situation that the two candidates with the highest unfavorable ratings in the polls are the ones we must decide between? Two people who both, in my opinion, pose a threat to this country if they are given the reins of power? Two people who many find untrustworthy?

I can't really speak for the Democrats, having never been a member of their party. I do know the Clintons wield a lot of power in the party and it may be that people felt Hillary was owed the nomination after losing it to Obama in 2008. That said, there are a lot of Democrats who don't like her and at least a few who won't vote for her.

Then we come to Trump. A man who doesn't refrain from nastiness if it suits his purpose. Who aired vicious innuendos about his opponents only to take them back when they backed down. What drives his support?

A lot of it is anger, as I've said in the past. The establishment, which is running the Republican Party, has turned a deaf ear to its more conservative members time and time again. Donald Trump has become a voice for some of these people. A way to express their dissatisfaction with the status quo. It may be cutting off their noses to spite their faces, but I suspect it's worth it to Trump's followers to see members of the party squirm.

So if this is the choice we're presented with in November, what are we going to do?

I can't tell anyone what to do, even if I had a decision here. And I don't. Yes, there is the concept of voting in "the lesser of two evils." But what do you do when either choice is unthinkable?

Do I want Hillary Clinton, who will continue to bankrupt this country morally and fiscally? Who is a person I disagree with on oh so many issues? Who I don't trust to tell the truth?

And then there's Trump. Do I want someone whose temperament makes me fear for our relationship with the rest of the world? Who is a smooth talker but doesn't seem to have a clue about what he's doing? Who I also don't trust to tell the truth?

It's the choice I never wanted to make. And now I face it.

We need to pray for wisdom for our country. I fear no matter what we decide, the country is going to lose. It's just a question of degree.

What do I do?

AN EVIL DAY

This is not a column I thought I would ever write.

If you hadn't heard, Wednesday a young man entered the south SunTrust bank here in Sebring and shot everyone there. He then apparently called law enforcement and told them, "I killed five people." Authorities raced to the bank and eventually got inside, where the alleged shooter surrendered without incident.

I happened to be out of town when this all happened. I learned about it while checking Facebook when Don Elwell reported what had happened. I was stunned. This is Sebring, for crying out loud. Mass shootings don't happen here, do they?

I admit my first thought was Don, whose office isn't far from the bank. A quick phone call assured me he was fine, but unable to get back to his office since the police shut down the area soon after he'd left to go to lunch. I was relieved, but still concerned about what was going on in my town.

One touching thing that came out of yesterday – the number of people, friends, and family, who called, messaged, or found another way to contact me to check on us and be sure we were okay. It was evidence that people care about us. Thank you to everyone who did so. I appreciate it more than you know.

I find myself stunned at this incident. I can't tell you how many times I've driven by that bank on my way to south Sebring. The victims could possibly be people I know. Someone in our small town chose to commit this atrocious act – here, where things like mass shootings aren't supposed to happen.

I have to commend so many for how they reacted to the unthinkable. County Commissioner Don Elwell kept people posted on Facebook with frequent updates on what was going on. Our police, fire, and rescue went above and beyond call of duty when faced with this crisis. We have good people here in Highlands County, and it showed yesterday.

I have no idea why the alleged shooter (I refuse to name him; he doesn't need the publicity) decided to do this. As I type this, no motive has been reported. And we may never know what was going through his mind that fateful Wednesday when he walked into the bank. All we know is five women are dead for no good reason.

We have joined the list of places in our country that have suffered mass shootings. It is a list that is too long by far. And given our toxic political climate, it's not a problem that will be solved anytime soon.

I wish I had magic words that could fix this whole mess. That could provide the perfect solution that would prevent another atrocity. Sadly, evil exists in the world, and it will show itself. Innocents will continue to be hurt. And I don't know how to keep it from happening.

To my fellow citizens here in Highlands County, I join you in solidarity and prayers as we travel this strange path. This one act, horrible as it is, is not who we are. We will prove that, I have no doubt.

To those outside of the county, don't judge us by this evil act. Support us and be patient with us as we sort this out. Don't see us as an opportunity to push a political agenda, but help us as we figure this out.

This wasn't supposed to happen here. But it did.

Let's be kinder to each other, hug each other, and look after each other. And let's try to figure out where to go from here.

Let's not let this one act keep us from being the best we can be.

TECH GOT UNDER HER SKIN

I am a woman who loves technology. I love living in this current time period, where it is readily available in all kinds of form. While I would have gotten along without it just fine 50 years ago (we still had books, after all), I'm happy to have it a significant part of my life.

Regular readers of my column may recall that I currently possess three laptops and a desktop computer (not counting what Don has). While to some this might be an embarrassment of riches, each computer has a reason for existing. While I admit some get used more than others (the MacBook is feeling neglected) I really don't want to do without any of them.

I wear a Fitbit, which tracks my steps. Like a lot of you, I own a smartphone (Android version). I use an iPad and a Kindle. I even have an old iPod I'd still be using if the battery hadn't up and died. (Yes, I could replace it. Don't tempt me further).

I say all that to reinforce that when it comes to tech, I am a soft touch. And while there is a lot of it I don't own yet, there are things I admit I eye with a little bit of longing.

My love of tech extends to the car I drive. My car is a 2006 Avalon, which includes an outdated GPS (the maps are from 2006, which means it can't always be trusted). When we bought the car, I had the radio adapted so I could plug my iPad into it and get music over the speakers. And it has a key fob.

Don can't be bothered with key fobs, so I happily took it. It allows me to unlock and lock the car from afar and pop the trunk with the press of a button. Press the wrong button and it will sound an alarm, which I have only done a couple of times.

It is an incredibly useful piece of tech. Two quick presses of the unlock button unlocks all the doors, handy when I have passengers. And if I forget to lock my doors and remember as I'm walking away, a quick jab at a button solves the problem.

However, my love of tech has its limits. There is a woman who has surpassed me, according to an article on www.foxnews.com. The article tells of one Amie Dansby, who recently had the chip to her Tesla model 3 vehicle implanted into her forearm. (The chip apparently unlocks and starts the car).

Dansby, a software engineer and programmer, describes herself as a "passionate technologist." She actually uploaded a YouTube video titled "Tesla Model 3 Chip Install – Warning There Is Blood" which shows her getting said chip, which was encased in what the article called a "biopolymer" (no, I'm not sure what that is) surgically implanted into her arm.

I saw the video. You can search for it on YouTube. Fair warning: she's not kidding about the blood.

Here's the amazing thing – this is not the first RIFD (radio-frequency identification) chip she's put into her body. She apparently has another one in her hand, which does weird stuff like open a browser on your phone and somehow interacts with her front door.

Does it work? Dansby reported to The Verge that it does, but not from a distance: her arm must be within an inch of the console. This seems to be a disadvantage to me, though I admit waving your arm to start your car sounds a little cool.

However, I'm really not looking to having anybody stick RIFD chips into my anatomy. So, I will have to be content with my tech items. Though Dansby does have one advantage over me – I bet she never loses her key.

BOLDLY GOING

We always remember where we were when we hear about a disaster. Saturday, I was actually still lazing in bed, thinking about getting up and starting my day when Don walked into the bedroom.

"There's been a disaster," he informed me.

Indeed, there had been. The space shuttle Columbia, scheduled to land in Florida that morning, had exploded or disintegrated in a bright Texas sky. As I type this, authorities still search for debris and answers, and we mourn the loss of seven men and women who dared to go to the stars.

In all the tears and honors for the dead, there has been a question: is manned spaceflight worth the cost? There is no doubt that the space program is tremendously expensive. Each mission costs hundreds of millions of dollars. It is not the safest way to travel, even though its track record is pretty good.

Some say it is not. They suggest that space travel would be cheaper and safer if it were unmanned. Some feel that traveling into space is a waste of time anyway, and that we should quit altogether. In their eyes, there are better uses for the money than to fritter it away on sending men and women into space.

If I get to vote in this, I would have to say that yes, it's dangerous. Yes, it's expensive. And yes, we have to keep exploring, in spite of all that. Quitting may save us some money in the short term, but we will lose in a lot of other ways in the grand scheme of things.

Exploration has always been fraught with risk. Many explorers have paid for their travels with their lives. Ponce de Leon, Ferdinand Magellan, Francis Drake, and Robert Scott are just a few such people. Do we wish they had not chosen to explore? Haven't we gained from what they discovered? If we asked them, would they say that exploration should cease because it cost them the ultimate price?

There are many arguments to be made for the continuation of exploration. One compelling one was made, interestingly enough, by a fictional character. It is fitting in regards to our topic, because it was made by none other than Captain James T. Kirk from the very first "Star Trek" series. In the episode "Return to Tomorrow," the Captain and his crew are discussing a mission. Dr. McCoy warns that it is dangerous. Kirk's response?

"They used to say if man could fly, he'd have wings. But he did fly. He discovered he had to. Do you wish that the first Apollo mission hadn't reached the moon or that we hadn't gone on to Mars or the nearest star? That's like saying you wish that you still operated with scalpels and sewed your patients up with catgut like your great - great - great - great - grandfather used to. I'm in command. I could order this. But I'm not ... because ... Dr. McCoy is right in pointing out the enormous danger potential in any contact with life and intelligence as fantastically advanced as this. But I must point out that the possibilities, the potential for knowledge and advancement is equally great. Risk. Risk is our business. That's what the starship is all about. That's why we're aboard her."

It behooves us to make spaceflight as safe as possible. We need to study what went wrong on Saturday and determine if we can keep it from happening again. We might even consider the prospect of moving beyond our current space shuttle fleet and finding a better way to travel in the great unknown.

But let's not stop going there. There are still things to discover. They will not be found by not going out there. The seven men and women who died on Saturday knew that. Let's honor them by living it.

FORGIVE THIS MUCH

Question to ponder today: how easy is it for you to forgive?

A lot of us would answer, "it depends on what the person did." After all, some offenses are easier to forgive than others.

I think about this regarding myself. Spill something at my house? No problem forgiving that. Forget my name? It would be hypocritical of me NOT to forgive that, since I do it often enough (I mean forget other people's names, I can usually remember my own). Cut me off in traffic? While that's a tough one for some people I can generally forgive that without wishing harm on the other driver.

But I will admit that there are scenarios for me where forgiveness is a lot harder. The biggest one? Family. You can go after me all you want, and in general I can forgive that. But if you go after my family... well, then we have a real problem.

And if you actually did harm to someone I love...my instinct would be to pay you back. I would certainly struggle with wishing you well. And forgiveness? That would be tough.

So I ask you for a moment to consider the family of Botham Jean, a young man who was killed by an off-duty police officer who says she mistook his apartment for hers. The case, which took place in Dallas, Texas, caught a lot of attention because Jean was black and the officer, Amber Guyger, is white.

According to the article I read on www.abcnews.go.com, Guyger was found guilty of murder. The same jury that convicted her proceeded to sentence her to 10 years in prison.

Not everyone was happy with that sentence. The District Attorney had suggested that she be incarcerated a minimum of 28 years – one for each year of Jean's life. Most of the victim's family seemed to feel it was too light a sentence.

But then there was Brandt Jean, the 18-year-old brother of Botham Jean. He took the stand (apparently after the sentencing) and spoke directly to Guyger.

He told her that "I love you just like anyone else." He said he forgave her and that if she went to God and asked Him, he would forgive her too.

The young man didn't look totally comfortable on the stand but pressed on. He said that he thought his brother would want the best for her, and he did as well. That the best thing would be for her to give her life to Christ.

Then, he asked the judge if he could hug Guyger. He wanted to embrace the woman who'd needlessly taken the life of his brother. Get that?

The judge granted his request, and in front of the judge's bench Brandt Jean embraced a weeping Guyger.

At this point in the video, I admit it got a bit dusty in my office.

Could you do that? Could you forgive the killer of your loved one and wish the best for them? Could you then embrace them and give them comfort?

I want to say I'm that good, but I don't know if I am. I don't know if I could sit there merely a few months or a year after the event and say I forgave the person and mean it. It would be hard. It would mean laying aside my own pain and being merciful to someone who didn't deserve it.

I hope I can become that kind of person. But I hope I never have to find out if I'm capable of that kind of forgiveness. Brandt Jean was, and for that he's my hero.

GRANDBABIES

When I first contemplated this collection, I knew there would have to be a grandabies section. My tales of Lavinia and Matthias are among my most popular columns. There aren't as many of them as there are of others, but they've only been around for five years or so.
Enjoy reading about my journey into grandmotherhood.

WELCOMING A BABY

As I type this, I am very tired. My schedule this week was totally disrupted. I spent a restless night on a couch and my good eating habits went out the window.

I am so happy I don't care about any of that.

I got the call from John on Monday while at a doctor's appointment myself. The doctors had decided to induce labor on Amanda on Tuesday, did Don and I plan on coming up?

I told him we'd get back to him with our plans and finished up my own appointment. Don was called soon after and we discussed the matter. Things were complicated by the fact that one of our cars was in the shop, leaving us with one vehicle to work with. There was also my mother-in-law to consider.

But we were determined so we came up with something. Don and I would drive up late Tuesday afternoon and Don would leave at some point in the evening. I would stay over and Don would return with his Mom sometime on Wednesday, and the three of us would come back to Sebring at some point.

I had to make plans to be away for at least 24 hours. Fortunately, I have understanding friends. They include the women in my Ladies Bible Class, which I managed to teach despite being very distracted.

Tuesday evening found me and my fellow grandma-to-be Alisa at Heart of Florida Medical Center an hour north of Sebring. They were just starting things with Amanda, and progress promised to go slowly.

After Don went home, the kids encouraged Alisa and me to go to their house nearby for some rest. Nothing was expected to happen before Wednesday, and if it did we'd be 15 minutes away.

Because I have pets, I got to sleep on the couch in the kid's den. John and Amanda have three dogs and two cats. Alisa got the baby's room. We said good night and bedded down for the evening.

Well, two of John's dogs decided that I couldn't possibly sleep on the couch by myself. Dax, the bigger dog, at some point thought I made a comfy mattress while Ollie figured my feet needed warming, though he moved up near my head at one point. The third dog, Luca, might have joined us had I realized he needed to be encouraged to do so. Instead, he sat nearby and watched all the shenanigans.

The next morning, after breakfast and much needed coffee, Alisa and I returned to the hospital. We found out that John and Amanda's daughter didn't like labor: her heart rate decreased while they were trying to induce. After a second attempt gave the same result, the doctors told us that they'd have to do a caesarean.

Amanda was quickly whisked away. John suited up and was soon taken to the operating room. Alisa and I sat and waited, maybe not as patiently as we could.

At 10:37 Wednesday morning, Lavinia Joanne Ware came into the world. She weighed in at six pounds and four ounces and was 19 inches long.

We got to see her less than two hours after she was born. She has a capful of hair that reminded me of her dad. Beautiful dark blue eyes and so light I could hold her all day and might have if I didn't have competition in that area.

Amanda and John understood and let us hold Lavinia and ooh and aah over her and take pictures, some which found their way to Facebook. In my humble opinion she's the most beautiful baby in the world, but I admit I might be biased.

Welcome, Lavinia. Know that you are already so loved by so many. I look forward to getting to know you and teaching you about important things, like God, reading, and chocolate.

So if you see me with a smile on my face this week, you know why. Join me in welcoming this precious girl to our world. Let's make it a good one for her.

A GRANDBABY COLUMN

One of the promises I made to myself when my granddaughter Lavinia was born was that I would not turn this space into an "All Lavinia, All the Time" place. I figured people might want to read about topics other than how cute my grandbaby is.

She turned 20 weeks old yesterday, and I think I've shown remarkable restraint under the circumstances. So get ready for a baby column. If that's not your thing, read the comics or something. I won't be hurt.

You have to understand something about me. When I see a baby, I go from an intelligent and coherent woman to someone who babbles in baby talk and silly attempts to win a smile. It is no different with my granddaughter. In fact, it's worse, because when she was born she quickly got attached to my heart.

In this grandma's opinion, Lavinia is an adorable baby. She has a heart-shaped face and a smile that would melt the stoniest heart. She's more than doubled her birthweight but, as a friend of mine said, she's still a little peanut. If she let me, I could hold her all day.

Sadly, she probably wouldn't let me. Lavinia is a momma's girl through and through. While we are at the point I can hold her for longer periods of time, there are other times only Mommy will do. And Lavinia will quickly make that known. Loudly, even.

I am blessed that Amanda posts pictures at least once a week of the baby so I can get my fix in. John and Amanda live a little over an hour away, which is far enough away that trips need to be set up. Thankfully, as long as they have notice, the kids are pretty good about letting us invade.

Their house is filled with cheerful chaos. You see, before they had Lavinia, the kids had three dogs and two cats. The animals stayed and have adjusted to the new little life among them. John believes that the dogs think she's a new member of the pack. They can be protective, hanging around her. That is not without its hazards, as one of them discovered when Lavinia got hold of his ear and pulled. But if I remember correctly, this particular puppy mangled one of her toys and licked her feet, so maybe this was payback. I'm not saying it was a good thing to do, mind you, but babies learn these rules eventually. She's only 20 weeks old, give her time.

Lavinia loves to be sung to, according to her mom. I am once again taking familiar tunes and making up my own words to them, just like I did when her daddy was young. I am working hard to earn smiles from her, because I am addicted to that toothless grin.

And I love watching my oh-so-serious oldest son interacting with his daughter. You have to know that at one point in his teenage years John swore he was going to be a hermit. But now, this young man who once posted a picture of a baby with nutritional information on its forehead (I am not kidding) plays and interacts with Lavinia in ways that move me deeply. Watching him is a treat in and of itself.

I was told being a grandmother was different from being a mom. All jokes aside, there is truth to the statement. I can't fully describe it, but there's a special tie between me and Lavinia. One I hope gets stronger as she gets older.

So that's my grandbaby column. I hope you enjoyed it. And fair warning – it probably won't be 20 weeks before there's another one. After all, there's a lot more I can say about my cute grandbaby. Talk to me if you want to hear it.

THEIR ROYAL ADORABLENESSES

A couple of weeks ago, I told you how my friend Dixie offered to take me to South Carolina to meet my new grandson and bond with my lovely 21-month-old granddaughter. I took her up on her generosity, and very early on a Thursday morning (if anyone questioned my love for my family the fact I got up and moving before sunrise should be ample evidence) we set out on the 10+ hour drive to Taylors, South Carolina.

It was a fun trip. Dixie and I shared stories about our respective families and talked about all kinds of things, including the horrible traffic on I-4 (we never figured out where all the cars came from). With stops, we didn't arrive in Taylors until after five in the afternoon.

Not long after we got there, I had the privilege of holding my almost 1-month-old grandson, Matthias. He reminded me of his dad when he was a baby – long and lean. In fact, I used to refer to John as my "long, lean, mean machine." Matthias may well inherit that title.

Words cannot describe the joy of looking into his deep blue eyes, holding him close, kissing the cheeks I'd only seen in pictures. It was worth bad traffic in Florida just for this.

And then there is his big sister, Lavinia. I'd last seen her at Thanksgiving, and she's already changed so much in that short amount of time. She talks more, interacts more, and is developing quite the personality.

I got to interact with her, playing games and making her laugh, which delighted me. She hasn't quite mastered the word "grandma" yet but I'm hoping that will come with time. She did like the gift I brought her, a blank journal for her to draw in. Lavinia loves to draw, and I figured giving her something safe to draw in would be a good thing.

Dixie took to my family with no problem except for one. Ollie, one of the kids' dogs, somehow got the idea Dixie was the devil and barked at her if she moved. Dixie in turn threatened to make him go play in traffic. Fortunately, both emerged from the experience unscathed.

We also got to interact with John and Amanda, which was a bonus of the trip. Several games of Scattergories were played to hysterical results. On Sunday we worshipped together and I got to hear John speak on Sunday night.

Because we were leaving early on Monday (again, before sunrise – the things I do for family), we said our goodbyes Sunday night. Lavinia gave us kisses and Matthias received his share of hugs and kisses from Dixie and me before they went off to bed. We swapped goodbyes and "I love yous" with John and Amanda and got to bed relatively early.

I got home around 5:30 PM on Monday very tired but happy. Dixie had helped make something important come true for me, and she has my deepest gratitude for her kindness.

I will see the grandbabies with Don in March. I know they will have grown. They will have changed. Who knows what words Lavinia will know by then? Will Matthias be awake longer?

Whatever. I'm looking forward to it. I love my kids, but I have to admit the royal adorablenesses that are my grandbabies are pretty special. If you're a grandparent, you get it. If not, just take my word for it. And if you see me, ask to see pictures. They're pretty great.

"I DON'T KNOW"

The above title is courtesy of my two-year-old granddaughter Lavinia. I asked her this morning what I should call my column this week, and that was her answer.

This week Don and I are in South Carolina, where my oldest son John and his wife Amanda live. We're visiting them and their adorable kids, Lavinia and 7-month-old Matthias. My other son James is here as well. It's quite the houseful.

And if you are concerned, let me assure you that Don and I took precautions when we traveled up here. We drove as opposed to flying. Our masks are in our car, ready to use. Not that we've gone anywhere. We're having too much fun here.

I have one of the best daughters-in-law on the planet. Even though neither she nor John drink coffee, she has a coffeemaker and coffee for me when I come. She has graciously allowed us to disrupt her schedule to a certain extent so we can spend time with the kids. Her husband isn't too shabby, either.

They even let us have the baby's room to sleep in, moving Matthias to their walk-in closet for the week. This gives us some privacy, a place to put our luggage, and a queen-sized air mattress.

If I had anything to complain about, it might be that mattress. I've yet to own an air mattress that didn't have a mysterious leak some-where, and this large one is no exception. It's a very slow leak, which means we can start off at night with a perfectly firm mattress only to find it somewhat deflated in the middle of the night. It's fairly easy to inflate again but having to do so at three or four in the morning isn't a fun way to wake up.

Despite that, we're having a blast. Lavinia has grown more talk-ative and interactive since we saw her in March. She still loves to be read to, which makes her writer grandma incredibly happy. She even "read" me a story, a moment I captured on video. It's precious.

Matthias is also more "with it." He loves to be sung to, and I've fallen back to my old trick of making up words to tunes I know. Right now he's teething, so his nights are a little rough sometimes. I've spent a bit of time rocking him in a recliner, crooning silly made-up songs to him and trying to win a wide smile from him. Tough job, but it comes with the title.

Mornings have fallen into a routine. Don or I are the first ones up. Lavinia wakes up and I go get her out of bed (her dad usually does this, but I let him sleep in). After a diaper change, she gets breakfast (sausage biscuits. She eats the biscuits and offers the sausage to Grandpa). After a while, the rest of the house stirs, and the day starts.

After the kids go to bed at night the adults usually play a board game. These can be quite entertaining. James and John are competi-tive when it comes to each other and watching them interact is almost as much fun as playing the game. Seeing how well the two brothers get along is something I've cherished – a parent wants the siblings to care about one another. They clearly do, and it's a good thing.

All in all, this has been a great week. One of the best things? To hear my granddaughter say, without prompting, "I love you, Grandma."

Out of all English sentences, that is probably my favorite.

ANOTHER GRANDBABIES COLUMN

Today I'm typing this from sunny South Carolina, where I'm spending time with my oldest son and his family. Well, to be honest, I'm spending a good deal of time with his kids, my beloved grandbabies.

Even though I get to visit with the kids via video chat every week, it's different to see them in person. Both are growing so fast and each are a delight in their own way.

Lavinia will be three in less than a month and is quite the chatterbox. I don't speak perfect Lavinia yet, but I get most of what she says. She takes after her mom in looks except for her hazel eyes, which came from Daddy. She has her cranky moments but usually is cheerful and loves to be tickled.

Matthias is nearly fifteen months old and a cutie. He is also very much a mama's boy, and there have been times that only Mommy would do. He's slowly warming up to us, letting me tickle him and kiss him and babbling quite a bit. In looks, he is definitely his father's son.

I love spending time here. The house, with its two kids, three dogs, and two cats has the feeling of barely controlled chaos at times.

But everyone is taken care of and happy, and John and his wife Amanda are doing a great job in raising their two youngsters.

When it comes to daughters-in-law, I lucked out. Amanda is so willing to let us disrupt their lives for a few days. Moreover, she encourages me through an exercise program I'm working on, even walking with me while I'm here. If I could kidnap her and the rest of the family back to Sebring I would.

The family takes a walk around the neighborhood every afternoon, weather permitting. Yesterday they tried Matthias out walking with a backpack on that had a leash. The theory was that they would let him walk and be able to keep him out of trouble.

The problem was, Matthias had strong opinions on where to go, and it wasn't always in the direction everyone else was going. John discovered he could lift Matthias off his feet with the leash and set him in the right direction, to all our amusement. In the end, we gave up and Amanda carried him the rest of the walk. But it was fun.

The kids love music, at least certain kinds of music. For example, I now have the song, "Baby Shark" firmly stuck in my head and can now sing the whole thing if necessary. It is a favorite around here. Other popular hits are "The Wheels on the Bus" and "Hush Little Baby."

Because of the pandemic, we don't go out very much. There is plenty to do at home, and Amanda is a great cook. John is a partial hermit anyway, and it's nice to chill a bit instead of running around.

Friday we'll say our reluctant goodbyes and head back to Sebring. I'll be a little sad, because I will miss this family that has so much of my heart. But part of me also looks forward to my own bed and my own environment.

Hold your family close. Enjoy them when you can. They are truly a blessing.

Until next time, John, Amanda, Lavinia, and Matthias. I love you all.

BEING GRANDMA

This week I have not been in Florida, enjoying our pleasant weather. I have been in South Carolina, where it is much colder, enjoying my grandchildren. Amanda, my daughter-in-law, is in Florida this week with her younger brother, enjoying some fun time together. I am here to make sure that the kids stay alive and John, my son, stays sane.

I have said in the past that I have a fantastic daughter-in-law, and this week gives me no reason to doubt this. Amanda left a freezer full of food and detailed directions on all meals, including snacks. She explained their routine to me and displayed confidence in my ability to manage. I still say John marrying her was one of the best decisions he's ever made.

The kids are, as always, a delight. Matthias is now two and talking a lot more than even a couple of months ago. He loves to be read to, and I've lost count of the number of books we've gone through – and it's only Wednesday.

Lavinia is cute and funny and has a smile that will melt your heart. On Sunday evening, John and I arrived a couple of minutes late to services (Amanda, who didn't leave until early Tuesday, was already there with the kids). We walked in on a prayer and waited in the back for it to be finished. When it was done, Lavinia, in a loud tone as clear as a bell, asked, "Can I play now?"

We all got a chuckle from it and I plan to file this tale under "things to embarrass my grandkids about" for when she's sixteen.

It hasn't all been sunshine and rainbows. Lavinia hates going to bed, and I usually leave John to fight that fight. I'm sleeping in Matthias's room (he's in his parents' closet in a Pack and Play) and I can hear her if she wakes up in the middle of the night. Or her usual early in the morning. As in, around seven in the morning.

Lavinia can also be stubborn. Today, I asked her to look for socks in her room, and she refused. I asked her if she was going to obey me, and she said, "No."

That's when she learned that Grandma could spank (Before you freak out, it was two swats on her bottom and thigh and not very hard). She cried, which is normal. We then hugged and talked about it because she needs to know that while I AM Grandma, and love her to death, she also must obey me.

But despite occasional hiccups, things have gone fairly smoothly. John, who works from home, has been able to concentrate on that while I attempt to keep the trains running on time. There are things that need work – the family room looks like a tornado hit it – but overall, we're doing okay. The house is still standing, and the kids are warm and fed.

I'd forgotten life with toddlers. They are a joy and fun, but when you're in charge they are also extremely tiring. You are constantly feeding and/or changing them, spending time with them, and checking on them when they're quiet and out of sight, as well as doing other unimportant things such as feeding yourself, getting some sleep, and, in my case, writing.

But I've managed to get this little column done while the kids sleep peacefully, so that's a win.

Will I be glad to get home on Saturday? Of course. I miss Don and it's home, after all.

Will I miss my grandbabies the minute I leave on Saturday? Of course. What else would you expect?

"OH, BISCUITS!"

I realize that the title of this week's column might be mystifying to my readers. Hang on, I'll explain.

As I type this, Don and I are in South Carolina visiting my oldest son John, his amazing wife Amanda, and two of the most precious grandchildren on the planet, Lavinia and Matthias.

Lavinia is fast approaching her fifth birthday. She is super bright, has a smile that will light up a room, and recently overcame potty training (no more diapers is a thing to celebrate).

Matthias is in the middle of potty training, a process most parents can sympathize with. He is usually okay during the day and can wear underpants if he's just at home. Going out or anytime he's in bed (naptime or bedtime) requires a pullup or diaper. But he's getting there.

While I was here Amanda got in some new underpants for him. She has to order them online because the child is skinny, despite how much he eats. Matthias, charmed by the new briefs, tried several of them on the day they arrived. I'm rooting for him keeping them clean and dry.

They aren't awful kids. But, like anyone else, they have their issues. Currently they are sharing a room while Don and I camp out in Matthias's room. Bedtimes have become an exercise in not going crazy.

One night we tried putting them to bed at the same time, reasoning they were tired enough to fall asleep right away. We quickly learned the error of our ways as they played together and did just about everything except what they were supposed to be doing.

After that debacle, we went back to putting Matthias to bed first, waiting for him to fall asleep, and them putting Lavinia to bed. This depends on Matthias settling down quickly, which is not guaranteed. But everyone is doing their best, I suppose.

While I have gotten to see them via video chats with Amanda every week, to be here in person is so much better. Both of them are so interactive and imaginative. Matthias especially has grown in his verbal skills, though with both of them you still sometimes wish there was an interpreter.

I have read numerous books with the two of them cuddled in my lap, had several tickle sessions involving wiggling, giggling grandchildren, and generally enjoyed watching them as they go about their day. Grandchildren are a precious thing. You can't tell me otherwise.

And John and Amanda, as always, have been welcoming and loving. They brush off any inconveniences our presence brings with a "we're happy to do it." They generally let us spoil their children and disrupt their daily schedule with no complaint. They have no idea how grateful I am for all of this, no matter how many times I thank them.

So, about the title to this week's column: it comes to us by way of Lavinia.

For reasons we can't figure out, she has started saying, "oh, biscuits" when something irritating or annoying happens. She says it in a light-hearted tone, and her three-year-old brother has begun to imitate her in this respect.

It's funny and if we laugh she'll grin. It's a lot better than other phrases she could adopt, so we're not too worried about it. It will probably fade in time.

I have a few more days to love and spoil before Don and I need to return home. I intend to do as much as I can before it's time to head to the airport. And then, when I hug and kiss them goodbye and head for the airport, knowing it will be months before I return, I just might mutter, "Oh, biscuits."

TIME WITH GRANDBABIES

I've been in South Carolina this week, visiting my beautiful grandbabies (and their parents as well). By the time this column comes out, Don and I will be on the way back to Florida.

The visit has been somewhat colored by the fact that everyone but Matthias has been coughing. Poor Amanda, my daughter-in-law, is dealing with an infection in both ears, which hasn't been fun. In spite of this, she has been a gracious hostess to us. Lavinia was laid low with a fever mid-week but will hopefully improve as she is medicated and cared for.

Lavinia is now five and preparing to start kindergarten in less than two weeks. This is a concept I'm sometimes struggling with – wasn't she a baby a few days ago? But she is even bigger than she was in March, when we last visited.

She is adorable, trying to fix her own hair in ponytails and able to unlock the front door using the keypad. She can't quite print her name yet, though she knows it starts with "L." Ask her where she lives and mama's phone number and she can spout both out.

I can usually help her overcome a bad mood by first waiting till she is calming down and telling her I don't want to see her "toothies."

She immediately responds with a giggle and a grin, and her world is back to normal.

Her favorite color is blue and she loves unicorns and her stuffed Lambie. We've spent time watching TV and playing Super Mario Kart on her daddy's computer.

Another thing she has shown an interest in are the pictures of her and Matthias I have on my computer and/or phone. We spent quite a bit of time one day going through all the pictures I have of them, separate and together. Some of them even got an "Aw" from her. It was special.

Both she and her brother still enjoy being tickled and read to. They play together more or less peacefully with only occasional flareups.

Matthias, at three, is more articulate than he was a few months ago. Sometimes I still have trouble understanding him but it's less of a problem now. He has gone backwards in potty training and is back in pullups. But he's three and I'm sure as he gets older he will conquer this skill.

He is a cuddler at times and a Matthias hug is a special thing. For that matter, so are Lavinia hugs. Kisses are prized.

Baby Shark is still somewhat popular but there are other cartoons as well. They like a tablet app called Homer which teaches things like letters and numbers, and includes videos about trucks, which both kids are big fans of.

We've had the opportunity to spend time with John and Amanda after the kids went to sleep. The conversations have been insightful even if we don't always see eye-to-eye. I look at my oldest son and sometimes wonder at the good, intelligent man he's become. Don and I are proud of him and Amanda, and so blessed they are part of our family.

Saturday, there will be hugs and kisses and some sadness at leaving this precious family. But I know they are merely a phone call away. And I hope that they are half as grateful for us as we are for them.

A HOT TIME WITH THE GRANDKIDS

I am now back home from South Carolina, where I spent an enjoyable week with my oldest son John and his family. Last week I talked about part of the visit – here is the rest of the story.

Thursday afternoon we ran into a problem: the air conditioning in the house up and quit. John and his wife Amanda were going out to dinner, but Amanda could control the thermostat through an app on her phone and promised to try and restart it while they were out. Don and I had grandparent duty, making sure Lavinia and Matthias got dinner and stayed alive while they were gone.

Unfortunately, the air conditioning did not respond to Amanda's attempts. We all contemplated that reality. South Carolina is not Florida, but it's not Maine, either. It was warm.

John offered to drive us to a hotel that night so we would be comfortable. Don and I thanked him for his kindness but said we'd experienced worse and would stay put.

That was not a lie. Don and I have been to Guyana, South America on mission trips and while our hotel room had air conditioning, the mission site did not and was quite warm.

Also, we'd stayed at the house when Irma came and pretty much wrecked our county's power grid. It took five very warm days to get our power restored and I learned the value of cold showers.

At least at John's house we had electricity and fans, both of which would be blessings in the next few days. Our biggest problem was explaining to Lavinia that she couldn't wear flannel pajamas to bed, as much as she loved them.

Friday two repairpeople showed up. The news was not great. The blower had died, and parts would have to be ordered to fix it. And it would not be an inexpensive fix.

John and Amanda took it in stride. Amanda declared she was not cooking and heating up the kitchen for dinner, so off we went to a great restaurant in Taylors called Lil Rebel Family Restaurant. Throwing weight loss to the wind I ordered a slice of chocolate cake for dessert, which I shared with two very eager grandchildren.

As I type this, the kids are still without air conditioning. My hope is that by the time you read this, it will be repaired and the problem solved.

But there's a takeaway I want to share with my readers. Let me explain that I was working on my lesson for Ladies Bible Class this week, which was on overcoming ingratitude.

While going through the book we are using, it occurred to me that during the whole situation, there was almost no complaining or whining from the adults in the situation. In fact, the common refrain from all of us was, "It could be worse."

And it could have been. The house has decent insulation, so while it was warm, it could have been warmer. We had windows we could open, and fans we could run. We could escape to an air-conditioned restaurant and eat dinner without sweating. The grandbabies mostly took it in stride, even if Lavinia had to forgo her beloved flannel.

The lack of complaining made the situation easier to bear. It spoke well of my son and his wife. Talking to Amanda today, they seem to be maintaining that good attitude.

While the loss of air conditioning was not an earth-shattering catastrophe, there are those who would treat it as such. And granted, none of us have health issues that were impacted by the warmth.

But what if we could have good attitudes even when things don't work the way we want them to? What if we focused more on what we have than on what we don't?

What if we could "rejoice always," as First Thessalonians 5:16 commands?

What would our lives look like?

Could it make a difference?

A GRANDBABY MILESTONE

Somehow, with life going on around here, I forgot to mention something very important: my granddaughter, Lavinia, started kindergarten on August 8th.

Yes, apparently she turned five on her last birthday and has now joined the ranks of the schooled. I say "apparently" because my memories of a much younger child are still very fresh in my mind. When did she get so big?

(As a side note, a friend of mine suggested that due to her age I could no longer refer to Lavinia as a "grandbaby." I made two points with my friend: One, she was technically correct in her assessment, and two, I didn't care.)

The tiny baby girl I got to hold the day she was born is now a long-legged cutie with large expressive eyes and a sweet smile. And to everyone's relief, she is enthusiastic about the concept of kindergarten, declaring the first day that she "loved it."

There have not been any tearful partings so far, and I pray there won't be. I have a searing memory of Lavinia's daddy at her age having to be pried from my leg one day because he did NOT want to go to school. Those are the kinds of memories parents would rather not have.

Things are a little different these days. Amanda drives Lavinia to school rather than making her take a bus, a decision I heartily approve of. To be able to be dropped off, Lavinia had to learn how to get out of her car seat by herself, something she mastered well enough to make me worry about other times she might decide to free herself. But so far, so good.

The first day of school wiped her out. I have an adorable video of Lavinia cuddling with her mommy and her Lambie (her beloved stuffed lamb she's had since birth), too tired to talk, only nodding now and then when Amanda would ask her stuff.

This quickly changed and when she gets home now, she's energetic and chatty. The house, which Amanda admits is quieter with Lavinia gone, is noisy again as my granddaughter interacts with little brother Matthias.

Three-year-old Matthias misses his sister during the day. That makes sense – she's been a constant around him all his life and her being gone for prolonged periods of time is unheard of. He's gotten a bit clingy with Mommy right now, something I hope he overcomes with time.

Amanda is doing preschool with Matthias, who is slowly warming up to the idea. It's good she has time to focus on him and help him grow. One day they were painting with apple halves, and Matthias didn't understand why he couldn't eat the apples he was painting with. Fortunately, Amanda somehow managed to keep him from doing so.

I've been through watching kids grow up before with John and James. Watching my grandchildren grow up brings back memories of seeing my own children grow and mature. And it's something we *want* to see – a child that never matures or grows up is not in a good place. Growing is a part of life.

But forgive me if I look back at the early days with fondness, and maybe shed a tear or two on their passing. I know the road ahead is filled with blessings, but I can't resist one last peek at what is behind. If I could, I'd give one last hug to the baby Lavinia was and then look forward to the amazing child she is becoming.

Here's hoping kindergarten continues to go smoothly for her.

PERSONAL

A number of my columns deal with my own life. Sometimes it's self-deprecating humor. Sometimes it's therapy because writing about something often helps me deal with it. Other times it's a celebration, like my anniversary columns which start off this section.

Here I've tried to layer dark and lighter columns. Unlike the previous categories, these are not in chronological order. So relax and prepare to take a peek at my life.

TWENTY YEARS

I first met him twenty five years ago, in Tampa, at a church service. He had turned 20 the previous September; I was less than one month away from it. He was involved in pre-med; I was just beginning college and working towards a teaching degree.

Were this a romance novel, I would say it was love at first sight. But it wasn't. Not that it was hate at first sight. We met and found ourselves running around with the same crowd of young people who like us were attending the University of South Florida and worshiping together with a congregation that made a point to reach out to the college community.

We went out together for the first time the fall of that year. We went with two other couples to see "Death on the Nile," and afterwards went out for ice cream. We started the journey of getting to know one another.

I found out that he was smart. We could talk about things and get deeply into subjects that sometimes left our other friends blinking in confusion. I also discovered something that was not obvious to others at the time - a wry sense of humor and a person who could laugh and enjoy himself with me at least.

Time passed. Two and a half years after we met he was accepted to medical school in Kansas City. While he was there we did our part to keep Ma Bell and the United States Postal service in the black. I remember standing by the two phones in the dorm halls, waiting for a call. I looked forward to them, and the letters we shared.

He asked me to spend Thanksgiving with him during his second year of medical school. While I was there he gave me an early Christmas present - an engagement ring. I almost didn't need a plane to fly when it was time for me to return to Tampa.

We were married on January 9th, 1983. Look at the calendar. Thursday will be our twentieth wedding anniversary.

We have gone through a lot in twenty years. The tail end of medical school. Numerous moves in four states, some which worked out better than others. The birth of two children and the fun and games involved in raising them. Frustrations within and without.

He isn't perfect, but I won't list his flaws in this column. His virtues are much more fun. Though he himself does not drink coffee, he knows how I like mine fixed. He is not above cooking dinner. His handling of our finances keeps us in the black while allowing me to indulge my book habit. He knows how to win a smile from me, or a laugh. He also knows when he needs to tell me to shape up and isn't afraid to do so.

As he often says, we make a great team. He's the organized one (I suspect he was born with a clipboard in his hand), the one who can make a plan and deal with the details. I am the people person, the diplomat. Over the years he has become more of a people person, and I have become a little more organized. It has worked out.

It's been twenty years, Don, since we together before God, friends, and family and promised, "For better, for worse, etc.". I can say without hesitation that you have fulfilled your end of the bargain. Thank you for making the "better" even more so and the "worse" not as bad as it could have been. Thank you for twenty years of being my best friend. God willing, this is still only the beginning.

Happy Anniversary.

30 YEARS AND COUNTING

1983. Ronald Reagan was President. Facebook wasn't even a gleam in anyone's eye. Gary Trudeau began a 20-month break from the cartoon series "Doonesbury." The world was quite a different place back then.

And on January 9th of that year a young man and woman stood up before God, family, and friends and promised to stay together till death do they part. For better, for worse, richer, poorer...you get the idea.

Don and me. We were a lot younger then we are now. Probably had a lot more stars in our eyes before reality brushed some of them away. But here we are. 30 years older and still together.

We've outlasted appliances, pets, and the economy's ups and downs. We've laughed together, grieved together, and occasionally yelled at each other. Yet even through the latter we've managed to keep it, and ourselves, together.

In this land of easy divorce, this feels like some kind of achievement. Especially since we're both still happy about being together and not just enduring. I'm not saying it's always sunshine and roses between us, but the good has far outweighed the bad over the years.

We complement each other in our gifts. Don is the level-headed one, the one who can keep us in budget and on the right track. He's the organized one that plans our trips and makes sure things more or less run well in the house. I'm the emotional one, the diplomat, the one who leads us to fun. I'm also the tech person of the house, who Don turns to when the electronics inevitably act up.

We've put the relationship to the test. We endured five moves in approximately five and a half years – believe me, that was a challenge and in my book fits into the "for worse" part of the marriage. We've had our sorrows. We've had our fights.

But at the same time we've had our joys. We've had the privilege of raising two wonderful sons. We have shared a lot of fun times, a lot of smiles and jokes.

How do we manage to stay together? I have to admit that we've been fortunate in that while we've had our bad times, they have never descended into the way of nightmares. We've always had God in sight, and I know that this has helped us during the darker times. We agreed a long time ago that no matter what, we would find a way to work together through the good times and bad.

It's meant putting up with each other's flaws. We've also had to learn to work around our differences. Don is a morning person; I'm a night owl. He's organized to a fault; my office looks like it was hit by a tornado. My temper is shorter than his, but when Don's temper is ignited, look out.

The world has changed over the past 30 years. Don and I have changed as well. We're older now, with two grown sons. We are hopefully wiser than that starry-eyed couple from 30 years ago and have a better understanding on what our vows mean than we ever did.

One thing that has remained constant and growing is our love for each other. I am grateful for that and know that it will only get better over the next 30 years.

Happy anniversary, Don. Thank you for 30 wonderful years. It will be a joy to walk the next three decades at your side.

33 YEARS AND COUNTING

This week I was saddened to learn that two friends of mine were ending their three year marriage. While I hope that they may find a way to reconcile down the line, at the moment they aren't together.

This got me thinking about my own marriage. It's been over 33 years since I stood in front of God, family, and friends and said "I do" to Don. Any way you look at it, that's a chunk of time.

I've been married longer than I was single. Longer than any job I've ever held down. And knowing how depressing the statistics are when it comes to marital longevity, I pondered just how we've managed to pull it off up to now.

I don't know how it works for you out there, but here's some random thoughts I had about marriage and making it last.

For one thing, we've managed not to kill each other in our sleep. Don't laugh – not killing your spouse is an important factor in making a marriage get to the double digits.

I must add that before I was diagnosed with sleep apnea and forced to use a CPAP machine, I snored quite a bit. Bless his heart, instead of shoving a pillow over my face Don resorted to earplugs.

And even though he snores, I have managed to sleep through it. So at this point we're both still breathing.

We've learned to accept each other, flaws and all. Don is resigned to the fact that I will never be mistaken for Suzy Homemaker. I deal with the reality that many of his socks that end up in the laundry hamper will be scrunched up. He is big on low-carb diets. I swear by Weight Watchers. He was born organized; I deal with life in a more scatterbrained fashion. We make it work.

We agree on the important things. We share a common faith. We also believe that Star Trek was and is amazing entertainment. And that reaching out to others is an important part of our lives.

On the other hand, we recognized a long time ago we didn't have to agree on everything. I love Mexican food; Don would prefer to stay away from it. I am a big fan of the TV series "Bones," but Don couldn't care less about it. And while friendships are ending all over due to the current election cycle we can disagree about aspects of it and still love each other.

We enjoy spending time together. Friday nights will find us in Battlezone at the mall playing Magic: the Gathering. We (mostly) enjoy the same kinds of movies. In Don I found someone I could have serious discussions with and also be silly with. We enjoy both kinds of interaction.

But we also give each other space. Don sometimes needs to be alone to deal with various aspects of his life such as journal reading or wrestling with the household budget. On the other hand I have this thing I do called writing which involves quality time with my keyboard or my jetting off to a workshop. We respect these compartments of each other's lives and do our best to accommodate them.

Maybe we're crazy. Maybe we're just out of step with the majority. But somehow we're making it work, one day at a time. 33 years and counting.

More people should be this nuts.

AFTER FORTY YEARS

This week was a momentous one in my life. This past Monday, Don and I celebrated forty years of being married.

"Celebrated" isn't exactly a good description of what we did. You see, on the day of our anniversary I was in Las Vegas, Nevada, attending a writing workshop. Don stayed home. When we discussed the situation, we agreed to postpone any celebration.

We did talk on our anniversary. And I posted something appropriately sappy on Facebook. But cards and the like are waiting for my return to Florida.

And it's an example of one thing I've learned over the years: the importance of being flexible. Don, bless his heart, knows how important my writing is to me and is willing to make accommodations for it. He is also not afraid to push me the days I gripe about writing and threaten to quit. We both know that we aren't restricted to a single day to celebrate our time together and are willing to make it work.

Another thing I've learned after forty years? To get to this point, you have to commit yourself to making the marriage work. Sometimes, it's an easy thing to do: other times it can be quite difficult and you find yourself struggling with this person that you love but maybe aren't too fond of at the moment.

A long time ago, Don and I agreed that no matter what happened, divorce wasn't an option. We could get mad at each other, argue, and maybe get pouty with one another (although to be honest Don doesn't get pouty, that's all me), but in the end we know that whatever isn't right, we will choose to fix it.

Not everyone likes this. True, there are situations where fixing isn't an option. But these are far rarer than a lot of people believe, at least according to statistics that place the divorce rate between 40-50% in the United States. Good news I discovered is that the divorce rate may be going down. That is encouraging.

After forty years you also realize that communication is important. It didn't take too long in our relationship to learn that neither of us could read minds, and sometimes we needed to talk things out rather than guess what the other one is thinking.

Oh, by this time we each have a clue about the other's opinion on certain things. But sometimes we need information from our partner to know what is going on. That means, for example, if there is an issue, not to stew about it and clam up. Don and I have found that if we can talk about something, we can deal with it most of the time.

And sometimes we have to agree to disagree. While we are on the same page on important matters, we don't always share the same opinions on given issues. These are not what I'd call, "Heaven or Hell" issues, but simply matters of opinion. By now we know that we can disagree and still respect each other.

Don is very considerate of me. Not only does he respect that fact I'm working on a writing career, but he also finds other ways to show he cares. For one thing, though he himself doesn't drink coffee, he knows how I like mine and will often get me some when we check out of a hotel. He has accepted that I'm not a morning person, though he sometimes forgets and tries to tell me something when I'm not entirely awake. But no one's perfect.

I am blessed to have had a wonderful marriage for forty years. I don't know if we can cram in another forty, but I'd sure like to try. I know the journey will be worth it.

HANGING UP THE PHONE ON SOLICITORS

L et me now confess to you a piece of my murky past. This is something I hesitate to bring up, because once it becomes public knowledge I am sure my reputation will suffer tremendously, perhaps to the point I'll be able to run for public office. What terrible revelation am I about to share? It's this: once upon a time, I - (dramatic pause) - was a phone solicitor.

It is not one of those jobs I display on my resume. My only excuse for it is at the time I was young and needed the money. I also comforted myself in the fact that we only called those who filled out a form that gave us their phone number. The fact that some of them forgot that they did such a thing when we called them was simply one of the challenges we had to deal with on the job.

Perhaps it is my former experiences on the job that helps me to maintain some rudimentary politeness when I am called by these people. That is not to say that I'm not tempted to slam the phone shut on their ears, especially when they choose to call when I'm in the bathtub, or in the middle of a long distance phone call. It's just that I manage to remember that phone solicitors are human beings too, and not a strange unlovable life form, and one of my guiding principles is to try to be polite to human beings, no matter how troubling they are.

This is bugging me particularly lately, because it seems that a number of these people have zeroed in on my phone number. Maybe it's that I've been home more than usual for the past few weeks, but I feel like I have been speaking to more than my share of these salespeople. It probably will do no good, but let me go on the record and state that the following calls will more than likely generate no income for those solicitors from me and my family:

– PHONE COMPANIES: Look, my husband and I gave careful consideration to which long-distance company to use, and we are not interested in changing it. Don't bother to tell me you are interested in saving me money. We both know your sole purpose is getting my money in your pocket. Don't act like you are some kind of philanthropist.

– POLITICAL CONTRIBUTIONS: I vote. I say nice things about the candidates I support. But asking me to give money is a risky business. One reason is that I have a poor track record in this area. Every time I have broken down and given money to a candidate, that candidate has subsequently lost the election. Please keep this in mind the next time you call.

– HAVE I GOT A DEAL FOR YOU!: This covers all magazine subscriptions, book clubs, time shares, and the like. Let me give you a deal. Quit calling me and maybe I will look into your product.

My mother had very little patience with phone solicitors. It didn't help that they would hear her deep voice and refer to her as "Mr. Helmers." Some of her responses to phone solicitations have become family legends. Once, a hapless solicitor called her and, referring to her as "Mr. Helmers" asked her if she might be interested in some aluminum siding.

"No thank you," she said. "My wife does all that for us."

She then proceeded to list all the qualities of this imaginary wife, concluding the list with a thankful sigh that she had found her. At this point I am sure the poor person at the other end of the conversation was only too happy to get off the phone and probably vowed never to dial our number again.

I'm sure some of you have some entertaining stories concerning phone solicitors. I'd love to hear them, so feel free to write or email me with these tales. But no phone calls, please.

ANYONE CAN HAVE A BAD DAY

In the interests of full disclosure, and so you understand where I'm coming from, I need to tell you that I suffer from anxiety and depression. I am in counseling, and I take my medications like a good girl and most of the time, that's enough to keep me on an even keel.

Most of the time. Not all of the time.

Today, it was as if my meds decided to go on vacation, or at least call in sick. All I know is I woke up feeling overwhelmed by stuff in my life, frustrated about my writing, and in general looking at my plate and seeing it overflow.

This would have been a day that it would be easy to blow off any and all of my obligations and curl up with books, video games, and chocolate. Shut myself up in my bedroom or office and only come out when I absolutely had to.

But among other things I deal with, I have an overdeveloped sense of responsibility that means if I'm expected to do something, I will do my best to get it done. Some days my best isn't that great, but I'll at least try.

So, after posting my woes on Facebook and asking for hugs, I put on my big girl panties, as they say, and did stuff. I managed to communicate with other human beings more or less effectively, and got things done that needed to get done.

It helped tremendously that throughout the day my post got a bunch of comments, offering hugs, kindness, and concern. They were little bright spots in the day that I needed to keep on going. That doesn't even cover the hugs and encouragement I got from people at my congregation during Bible study tonight. If you were part of any of that, thank you. It helped.

Someone may think, "But she says she's a Christian. Christians don't have bad days, do they?"

Um, yeah. We do. Just like anyone else. We have more tools to deal with them than a non-believer, but we have our share of unhappy times. And times when we need to lean pretty hard on others.

If you know someone who's having a day like I'm having, please be kind. Don't tell us to "just snap out of it;" believe me, we would if we could. Don't accuse us of lacking faith – Elijah, a man of great faith, got depressed to the point of wanting to die (you can read about it in First Kings 19). God didn't accuse him of lacking faith or tell him to snap out of it – He gave the man time to recover and then gave him something to do.

What can you do if a friend is going through a rough time? Hugs if they want them. An ear if they need to talk, a shoulder if they need to cry. If they need someone to help carry their load, be that someone if you can. Let them know you're in their corner, and they are not alone.

Chances are tomorrow I'll feel better. I'll have a better perspective on things, figure out how to manage what I must manage, and hope-fully tease out the knot in my current short story. The world won't seem quite as huge, and I won't want to retreat.

And things will be fine. Until the next time they're not. But I'm blessed to have people on my side who will be light in the darkness. So, I'll keep on going, thanks to them.

LEFT FOOT RIGHT FOOT

By the time you read this, I will have further evidence that I'm not a sane individual. This requires some explanation, so read on.

I will be in Las Vegas, attending a writing workshop. This alone does not qualify me for insanity, except that writers are a little crazy by definition. But there is something else going on the weekend I am there.

One thing I didn't know about Vegas is that there is some kind of running event almost every weekend. One of them takes place while I'm there, called The Color Run. It is so named because at the end of the race people get to throw colored powder at you. I am not kidding.

Anyway, one of my workshop buddies mentioned the 5K run and asked if anyone wanted to participate. Another attendee checked and found out you could walk it and it wasn't timed.

This is where the insanity started. I asked how fast she was planning on walking. She thought she could do the 5K (3.2 miles for most of us) in about an hour.

"Three miles in an hour? That doesn't sound too hard," I thought.

Okay, stop laughing out there. I know better now.

Before we go on, I must confess that I am not one that is an exercise lover. I write, which for me means sitting down a lot. Most of my exercise normally consists of navigating Walmart, which can give me a lot of steps if my Fitbit isn't lying.

Despite the previous paragraph, I decided I would give this 5K a shot. Crazy? Yes.

It occurred to me last week that maybe I should practice walking before the actual event. With Google's help Don and I determined that from our house to the end of our road was .6 miles. A round trip was therefore 1.2 miles, something that would be a good start for couch potato me.

So early one morning I got up, dressed for the occasion, and took off walking. My body, not used to this intense of activity, set up a protest. Unfortunately for it, I overruled discomfort and plodded on.

When I finished, sweaty and sore, I checked my time and realized I was walking a lot slower than three miles an hour.

Subsequent days improved my time, but not enough. Panicking, I messaged the gal who'd brought the walk/run to my attention. Should I drop out? What if I took too long? Maybe I was stupid for even trying this?

Her response was warm and encouraging. No, I shouldn't drop. I should just give it my best shot. Yay that I was training, even if I did start late. It was all good.

Encouraged, I continued to walk, and promptly strained a tendon, which meant some downtime at my husband's direction (when you're married to a doctor, they tend to do stuff like that). But I've continued to work at it and armed with a walking cane (in case the tendon acts up again) I plan to be at the starting gate, bright and early on Saturday morning.

Will I finish? Don't know. Depends on how I do. Right now, my goal is not to embarrass myself. If that means bowing out early, that's what I'll do.

So next week I'll tell you all about my experience at my first 5K. Until then, be well, and save a seat on the couch for me.

A COLORFUL RUN

Well, I didn't embarrass myself.

Last week I told you of my plans to walk my first ever 5k (3.2 miles) at an event called the Color Run. It is so named because at various intervals people through colored powder at you (last week I said it was only at the end of the race. I was mistaken).

So, when I got to the writing workshop I'm attending, I got in touch with Julie, the woman who'd gotten me and others together on this. Julie, in addition to being a writer, is a serious runner. As you will see, she is also an angel.

We agreed to meet at 7:00 AM on Saturday morning. There turned out to be five of us. I was the rookie, the others having run before. We set out for the starting line, a fifteen-minute walk from our hotel.

While we waited for the race to start, I asked Julie where we'd meet after the race, figuring she and the others would run ahead. She informed me she was walking with me instead of running to keep me company and encourage me.

When I protested, she pointed out that if I'd invited her to church, I wouldn't leave her to her own devices. She was not going to leave me on my first 5k.

There was a lot of energy in the air while we waited to start, and it was contagious. I started getting more excited than apprehensive. This could be fun.

We finally got to the starting line and the walk began. Patricia, one of my fellow writers, decided to run, but the other two, Kelly and Ranveig, joined Julie and me in walking down the Vegas streets.

Julie made sure I was breathing and doing okay. When I finally admitted I needed to take a shortcut (I was worried about how long I was taking) she asked me if it was okay if she and the others ran on and met me down the road? I said sure and turned onto a road connecting the run while she and the others took off.

I haven't talked a lot about what I saw on the walk. It's not that there wasn't anything interesting – it's that by this point of the walk I was concentrating on walking. That and getting sprayed at various color stations. My arms took the brunt of it, and I was sporting blue, green, and other shades as I got closer to the finish line.

Julie, Kelly, and Ranveig caught up with me and we pressed forward. Just before we got to the finish line, we had to cross a bunch of soap suds that came to our knees. And then, we strode across the finish line where medals waited for us.

Julie kept telling me she was proud of me and insisted on buying me a mocha latte to celebrate. I must admit I was proud of me too. All told, I ended Saturday with over 13,000 steps and a huge sense of accomplishment.

Will I keep walking? Yes. It's hard to say no to that now since I've proven what I can do. I'm already thinking of keeping it up so the next time a 5k comes up, I can walk it without the need for a shortcut. Something that I hope encourages you if you've thought about something like this but held off on actually doing it.

After all, if I, a 62-year-old couch potato can get to this point, who can't?

LET THE DOGS OUT

As I type this, it is Thanksgiving eve. I am almost totally prepared for the feast that will be held at the Ware household tomorrow.

The turkey is thawing in the refrigerator. The cranberry sauce is chilling. Two wonderful daughters-in-law are providing dessert, mashed potatoes, and sweet potato casserole. We will have a total of eight humans at the house, all ready to feast on the huge amounts of food that will be produced.

We will also have six – count 'em, six – dogs at the house to enjoy the day with us.

Six is actually a record for us. I think the highest canine population we've entertained before now is four, which has its good and bad sides. Given we are upping that number by two, I admit I'm doing some praying.

Let me take a moment and introduce you to the menagerie that will be gracing my home sometime tomorrow:

First, there's Barney, the main dog. He's a ten-year-old beagle that came to us via the Humane Society. I've written occasionally about his antics, including an unfortunate fondness for socks. He also likes ham and popcorn and will sell his soul (or at least enter his crate) for a taste of either one. He is the oldest dog of the bunch.

Hobbes wins the biggest dog category – we think he's part Lab but we aren't sure. He is large enough to hop over the gate my youngest and his wife set up in the doorway of their room to keep the other dogs out. Hobbes is very friendly, and quite possibly the youngest dog of the pack. He came along with youngest and his wife and has more or less fit into the craziness around here.

Gerry is our latest resident, part Jack Russell Terrier and Part corgi. He's Paul's dog. Tiny, he was initially wary of Hobbes but the two of them seem to have achieved an understanding. He takes anyone knocking on a door as a potential threat and barks sharply as a warning to us.

Those three live with us. Tomorrow, my oldest and his wife will come, bringing their three dogs. Their three consist of the following:

Dax, a graceful looking dog who's smaller than Hobbes but taller than Barney. He was the first dog John and Amanda owned. He was also the dog who managed to get some turkey off the counter one year, but we've forgiven him for that.

Ollie is a small brown dog who loves John, Amanda, and Paul, tolerates the rest of us, and hates the world. When you first meet Ollie your best bet is to ignore him until his curiosity outweighs his hostility and he comes to check you out. He and I have a pleasant relationship – he loves my office chair and will also sit in my lap. He overflows with personality.

Luca is a timid ball of fluff who is quite cute. When he's at my house he has to wear a diaper (I am not kidding) because for some reason he thinks he has to mark everything in sight at my house.

You may be wondering how we're going to handle things like dinner with six dogs running around the house. So far my evolving plan involves pressure gates at strategic locations and use of our large, fenced in backyard. Hopefully, we'll be able to eat without dogs in our laps.

Yes, it'll be chaotic. Yes, it'll be insane. And there will probably be at least one mishap involving a four-footed creature.

Of such lovely memories are made. And I am thankful for it.

CANINE CHAOS

Readers of last week's column might be curious to know how my Thanksgiving went. Last week I reported that our home was going to contain eight people and six dogs (That's right, six). Some of you might be wondering: did anyone snap? Did the dogs all get along? Is her house still standing?

I am happy to report that the holiday meal went off without a hitch. We had a lot of good food and a great time together. As far as the dogs are concerned, for the most part everyone got along and no one got hurt.

We did, however, employ the use of pressure gates so we could eat our meal in relative peace. This worked for all but Hobbes, the biggest dog, who could leap over the gates for the most part. Fortunately while this made the other five jealous, he did not interfere with our eating.

As you might expect, with six dogs under one roof, it was noisy. Very noisy. Loud to the point I half expected our neighbors to come banging on our door to complain.

Said banging would've increased the noise level since Gerry, the smallest dog, is compelled to bark whenever someone knocks on a door or rings a doorbell. It doesn't even have to be a REAL door or a REAL doorbell – just hearing it on the television is enough to set him off.

Aside from the noise and the occasional grumble or growl, everybody got along and, as I said, no one got hurt. On Thanksgiving.

Then came Friday...

I had just left the Verizon store after running an errand. Sitting in my car, I was talking on the phone to Don about what our plans were for the evening when he told me our youngest son was calling to him from the other end of the house.

I soon learned that the reason James wanted his dad was that our dog Barney and his dog Hobbes had gotten involved in an altercation involving food. Specifically, turkey drippings that had gotten within their reach.

The altercation between the youngest and oldest dog of the house was brief but fierce. Barney got the worst of it and was bleeding from puncture wounds in one of his floppy ears.

When I arrived home, the chaos had somewhat settled down. Barney was in his crate, blood on his muzzle, his ears, and his head, Hobbes was corralled, and James was cleaning blood from the walls. Given that Barney was still bleeding, Don and I knew our evening's plans were out the window. We were going to the vet.

Because it was after hours we had to travel almost an hour to get to an all-night vet clinic in Dundee. We put trash bags on the back seat of the car and hoped for the best for the interior. Barney tolerated the trip well enough, though he clearly wasn't a happy dog.

(You might ask why we didn't try to deal with the bleeding ourselves. Short answer: we like our hands and fingers unmarred by bites)

The vet was a wonderful lady who, with the help of techs and a muzzle, got Barney cleaned up. We were sent home with medication and Barney got a cone to wear around his head to keep him from messing with his wounds.

The cone was supposed to stay on a week. It lasted 48 hours. But he seems to be healing up nicely from his ordeal. And he and Hobbes are back to being friends again so apparently all is forgiven.

If only humans could be like that...but that's another column.

AFTER IRMA

It's Wednesday. I'm sitting in a room in Highlands Regional Medical Center's ER, watching over my mother-in-law. She's here because she suffered a seizure due to her electrolytes becoming unbalanced. The imbalance is no doubt due to the fact she's been in a house with no air conditioning (due to no power) since Sunday night.

As I type this, I'm not sure when or how I'll get the column to the newspaper. Normally I simply email the finished product to Romona Washington and cross it off my to-do list. But at this point in time I have no Internet access. I guess in a pinch I could type this out on my phone, which has wonky access, and then email it. If you're reading this now, I somehow figured it out.

Welcome to my world post-hurricane Irma.

Laying aside the fact of my mother-in-law's condition, I have a lot to be thankful for. Yes, we don't have power and it looks like days before that gets repaired. But we got through the hurricane with no one hurt and only minor damage to our property. The house, though it's currently uncomfortable to be in, is still standing.

Probably the worst thing we had to deal with was a live oak that fell behind Don's car in the driveway, barely missing the vehicle. It blocked his and Paul's cars until Tuesday, when our lawn man came and helpfully got it out of the way.

We have a baby generator that we're using to preserve our refrigerator items and charge our cell phones. We have food. We have a charcoal grill that a former resident of our home left here that has proven invaluable. Lanterns and flashlights light the way for us in the darkness. And thankfully, we have plenty of chocolate.

We'd prepared for Irma like we'd never prepared for a hurricane before. Any thoughts that we overdid it went flying out the window Sunday night when those hurricane force gusts blew against the house. In fact, there are things I wish we'd thought of beforehand, things we are missing as we go through day to day.

There are things that are gold now that pre-Irma we took for granted. Charcoal. D batteries. Lighter fluid. Who knew we should've stocked up on these? Once those things become available again I am sorely tempted to get some to lay by in store just in case.

But there are plenty of things we do have. Running water, even if we can't drink it, makes for washing dishes and hands. Because we filled up both cars ahead of time, we can get around to a certain extent, even if driving down U. S. 27 is more of an adventure than usual (note: when the traffic lights are out, you're supposed to treat the intersection as a four-way stop, NOT as a game of chicken.). We are merely suffering inconveniences, while others are going through far worse.

Right now my biggest concern is my mother-in-law getting healthy. Yet even in this I can be thankful, because in spite of not feeling well she will probably be more comfortable in the hospital where there's electricity and air conditioning than at home. And I know they'll take good care of her for us here.

I hope everyone reading this who was affected by Irma can find at least one thing to be thankful for. And I really hope you get to read this column – even if I wind up typing it out on my phone.

FROM COUCH TO 5K

Those who know me will testify to the fact that I am not athletic. In fact, I am so out of shape that if the zombie apocalypse ever happens and our lives depend on our ability to run, the best I can hope for is that people will say nice things about me at my funeral.

It doesn't help that my career does not encourage moving much besides my fingers. Writing is (usually) done from a seated position and sitting does not burn as many calories as walking or running.

I know of some writers who write standing up or even while walking on a slow treadmill. While it's possible I might write standing – until my feet started hurting, anyway – there is no way I am coordinated enough to type and walk at the same time. So, you can cross that off as a way to get me moving.

Out of shape is not good. It raises my risks for all kinds of bad stuff. But getting me to do something besides moan about it is tough.

Then along came my wonderful daughter-in-law, Amanda Ware. She told me about a program she was doing called Couch to 5k, which took you from couch potato to maybe running a real 5k.

Amanda was dedicated to this. She has two children under the age of 4, as well as three dogs and two cats. She found the time to do the program and even exercised during her off days. I was impressed.

And I was curious. Could the program work for someone like me?

One problem that had to be addressed was that I don't run very well, as in, at all. In fact, I have discovered to my dismay my body has literally forgotten how to run. So, the best I could do with the program was a power walk.

Amanda assured me the program would work fine under those conditions. So, one day I downloaded the Zenilabs version of Couch to 5k and decided I would give it a shot.

The program lasts eight weeks and you do it three times a week. I decided to try for early morning so that it wouldn't be too hot. That in itself was a change for me because no one would accuse me of being a morning person.

The program started easily enough. It swapped power walking with regular walking and only lasted 30 minutes. Gradually it increased in difficulty.

Then one day it jumped up to a full twenty-minute power walk. I admit when I saw that on Thursday (the walk was scheduled for Friday) I panicked a little. Could I really do 20 minutes without a break? Me?

A call to Amanda assured me. The program had been building me up for this, she said. I could do it. She had faith in me.

The next day, aside from two stops to tie loose shoes, I did the twenty minutes. I got a "good job" from both Amanda and my granddaughter, which meant a lot.

I continued the program while in South Carolina, Amanda going out with me to walk with me and cheer me on. She made it bearable, and I threatened to kidnap her back to Sebring. If I ever need a motivational coach, I know who I'm calling.

Last week I completed the program by doing a full thirty-minute power walk. Yes, I actually did that. Granted, I'm not the fastest power walker on the block. But that didn't matter.

And this week? I started a new program – Couch to 10k. By the end of it, I should be able to power walk for a full hour.

And after doing the first program I know better than to say it won't happen. It's entirely possible. I just have to stick with it and not give up.

So, if you're in the neighborhood and see a slow power walker trudging along, give her a cheer. I'll appreciate it.

A WEIGHTY TOPIC

Hi, I'm Laura (Hi Laura) and I am overweight.

I have regaled you readers with my attempts to lose weight. Currently I'm doing a second go round with Weight Watchers, which I have to admit has worked for me in the past and is helping me lose the weight slowly. As I type this, I'm 50 pounds lighter then I was two years ago. While I still have weight to lose, I'm kind of proud of what I've done so far.

Recently I've been following the posts of someone who calls herself "Your Fat Friend." She is apparently very overweight and all about fat acceptance and people not judging her because she's fat.

There's a lot she writes that I can get behind. Putting someone down because of their weight is simply wrong. Making assumptions about why a person is fat is risky. Giving unsolicited advice out of the blue is usually rude.

I know that I should get past my own reservations about how I look. There's a reason there's no picture of me with this column – for the longest time I hated having my picture taken. I thought I looked horrible, despite reassurances from people around me that I was mistaken.

I'm getting to the point where I no longer flinch at a camera. I can look at a picture of me now and think "Not bad," instead of "Ewww." But it's been a long time coming.

The tv show "What Not to Wear" had a saying – "Love the skin you're in." I think My Fat Friend believes that, and I see the point of it. Self-hatred benefits no one – not you, nor those around you.

No one should be made to feel like less of a human being because they don't fit in the right slot on a height/weight chart. I think My Fat Friend is right about that and I feel bad when I read of her experiences with total strangers mocking her because of her weight.

But...sometimes, when I read her posts, I feel guilty about trying to lose weight. As if I'm letting down a fat sisterhood by attempting to leave it.

Is it so wrong that I want to make myself thinner? It's not all vanity – I understand I was flirting with health issues when my weight passed the 200 pound mark. Getting down to a healthy weight will help reduce my risks for those issues.

I'm taking my time with it, because I know I'm making lifestyle decisions and I have to make sure I can still incorporate chocolate in this. That's okay with me. I didn't gain the weight overnight, so I don't expect to lose it quickly.

(And let me take a quick moment to plug Weight Watchers. They have never made me feel bad for gaining weight while on the plan and are all about accepting yourself and seeing yourself as someone beyond the numbers on a scale. They have helped me a lot.)

My Fat Friend has chosen to be content where she's at. I'm not going to sit here and tell her she's wrong. I know very little about her life, except what she's shared. I am neither her parents nor her God and have no say in how she conducts herself.

But I am not content. And I want to change. Why does a part of me see that as a betrayal to people like My Fat Friend?

PERKY CROSSES THE RAINBOW BRIDGE

W ay back in December of 1998, I wrote a column titled "Perky Finds a New Home." It told the tale of the energetic beagle puppy we'd brought home from Tampa and welcomed into our lives.

Over the years Perky became part of a number of columns I wrote. It's kind of an occupational hazard that comes with living with me. If he objected to how he was portrayed he managed to keep it to himself, though maybe it explains some of the so called "accidents" that happened on occasion.

Perky became my living doorbell. Someone merely had to approach the front door and my beagle would start baying, letting me know that someone was on the property. Sometimes it seemed that someone only had to think about approaching the door before he started his howling. Or maybe he sensed a random air molecule wanted to get inside the house and decided to let me know about it.

Perky enjoyed people food when he could get it. When I started using a meat slicer, he quickly learned what it sounded like and would come into the kitchen when he heard it running. He'd stand next to the counter, hoping for meat dropping on the floor, knowing that if he was patient I would feed him scraps from the slicer. I always made him sit first but his patience was always rewarded.

We had to watch him if we left food lying around. Once, when my younger sister was visiting, I had to leave a piece of chocolate cake unattended while dealing with something. She swears Perky was calculating how to outsmart her and get to the cake. Thinking quickly, she outsmarted him by covering the cake with a bowl. But it was a near thing.

At some point I learned Perky liked coffee – or at least my coffee. He would get into my office chair and lap up any coffee left in my cup. At least once he rested his paw on my computer keyboard while there, and I am forced to wonder if he was surfing the Web when I wasn't around.

As Perky got older, he was forced to slow down from his busy ways. Arthritis and a heart condition curtailed his activities to a certain extent. When John and Amanda came to visit with their three excited puppies, Perky would regard them as an old man might view rambunctious children in his presence.

One weekend, he appeared to have some sort of stomach upset. When medicine didn't resolve it, I brought Perky to the vet. After an examination I was given devastating news: a fast growing tumor, squashing his intestines. Surgery was ruled out due to his heart condition. It was a matter of time.

We worked to make the next few weeks as comfortable for Perky as we could. I cooked him rice and chicken, two things he appeared to be able to eat. We silently cleaned up his messes as he was unable to get outside in time. He grew thin and weak in spite of our efforts.

He took to lying in my office when I was in there, wanting nothing more than company. Then the day came that he didn't have the strength to move from my office to the kitchen, and he refused to eat or drink.

I kept watch over him as he seemed to fade before my eyes. One day, weary, I went to take a nap while he lay in my office. In that hour, Perky breathed his last and left to wait for us at the Rainbow Bridge, leaving a sad family to mourn his passing and rejoice in his long life.

(The "Rainbow Bridge" is a poem about pets that leave this life. Google the term to find it. Be prepared to sniffle.)

A NEW FAMILY MEMBER

R eaders of this column know that last year we had to say goodbye to our old beagle Perky. Age and health problems caught up with him, and he crossed the Rainbow Bridge peacefully at home.

After our initial grief had passed, the question came up concerning another pet. While we were not opposed to the idea, the time didn't seem right. Life was going on, and whenever it came up something seemed to say, "not yet."

Summer gave way to fall, fall turned into winter, winter became spring, and before we knew it summer had returned. It was about 11 months since we lost Perky. While we still have our two insane birds, there was no four-footed critter roaming our home, except for the visits from my John and Amanda's three dogs.

Last week I was roaming Facebook, as I often do, and I came across a picture of Barney.

According to the blurb accompanying the picture, Barney was an eight-year-old beagle available for adoption at the Highlands County Humane Society. He was friendly and sweet, and needing a good home.

I'm not sure what drew me to this – maybe because he was a

beagle, maybe because the blurb encouraged me to come and shake his paw – but I found myself thinking about him over the next couple of days.

I talked to Don. He reminded me that any new dog would mean more work for me, but he was interested as well. We agreed I would learn more and we'd consider it.

I called the Humane Society and talked to a very nice lady about Barney. I learned that he'd been found near the Miami aquarium and had hung out there long enough that he'd been named "Free Willy." A volunteer from the local Humane Society rescued him and brought him to Highlands County. Somewhere along the line his name was changed to Barney.

He sounded like a great possibility for us. I wasn't afraid to adopt an older dog. In fact, an older dog had some advantages in my book, including maybe being housebroken already. I'm no spring chicken myself.

As I drove down to the Humane Society, I called my mother-in-law to let her know I might be bringing someone home. She missed Perky as much as we did and was hopeful that Barney would work out.

When I arrived, I was directed to the kennel Barney was in. The first thing I noticed about him was that while other dogs were jumping and barking as I went by, he sat quietly, waiting for me to approach.

Once he was out of his kennel, he was more energetic. As I crouched down to say hello, he greeted me so enthusiastically he knocked me on my butt. I didn't hold that against him.

We seemed to be a good fit. I walked him about a bit and talked to Don some more on my cell phone. We both agreed that Barney had found his home.

A few pages of paperwork later, Barney and I headed for home. When we got there, he began to sniff out every corner of the place. His meeting with my mother-in-law went well, and in less than a week we are falling into a comfortable routine together.

He's not perfect – we are going to discover if you can indeed teach an old dog new tricks. But so far we've avoided most catastrophes (though we discovered I hadn't put all my coffee out of reach – we need to dog-proof the house again). He's sweet and loves to be petted. And we all feel lucky to have him.

I've mentioned the Humane Society a lot in this column. They were great in helping Barney and I find each other. Check them out at http://humanesocietyofhighlandscounty.com/home.html. Tell them Barney and I say hi.

MORNING PEOPLE VS. THE REST
OF US

I have a request to make of the morning people of the world. Nay, a plea, coming from the bottom of my sleepy heart.

Could you please cut the rest of us a little slack?

Somehow, the morning people got control of the world and life runs on their schedule, to the dismay of the rest of us. Oh, yes, I know: we were sleeping at the time they took over. Actually, I'm sure some of the more tender-hearted ones tried to wake us up; we probably just snuggled deeper into our blankets and muttered, "Five more minutes, please."

No one in their right mind would refer to me, or my two sons, as morning people. When I finally get out of bed (during the school year I am forced out at a horrible hour - as someone in my family used to say, "The birds aren't even up yet!") I resemble one of those zombies in an old 50's movie, staggering around barely managing to avoid the furniture. My kids are the same, and if I were awake enough to get a look at us I'm sure we are pretty funny.

After I get my first cup of coffee down, I begin to resemble a normal human being. Before that, though, all bets are off. Don has learned not to tell me anything important before I am out of bed and have had caffeine, even if my eyes are open and I have uttered words before then. He, of course, is a morning person, which I think they teach in medical school. I have yet to meet a doctor who was not a morning person to a certain extent. It's a good thing, too. Don can be roused from a sound sleep by a jangling phone and not only understand the doctorspeak they rattle off to him but actually give proper instructions in the same language. If I have to answer a phone from a sound sleep, it takes at least 5 minutes for me to understand basic English.

People like me used to be called "night owls." Our brains fully click on sometime after lunch, and we are just getting started come 9:00 PM. In my idea of a perfect schedule, I'd stay up and bang on my computer til 1 AM or so, and sleep until 10. If my oldest had his way, he'd stay up til 4 AM and sleep until noon. Unfortunately, the world looks down on such a wonderful life, and keeps forcing us into the "get up at the crack of dawn" crowd. "You could become a morning person if you wanted to," they tell us. Morning people all think their way is superior and that it is simply a matter of will.

Tell that to my body. It fights an early morning rising with every molecule. Day after day, my mind and body have an argument. "We have to get up!" the mind says. "Why?" asks the body. "Because the alarm clock went off!" states the mind. "What does IT know?" argues the body. The body is smart - it realizes the longer it can engage the mind in a debate, the longer it can put off actually getting out of the bed.

Of course, some people suggest the answer to becoming a morning person is going to bed early. I try to do that, but often my brain does not realize we are supposed to be shutting down and refuses to quit, spinning all kinds of stories, potential column ideas, and what I really should have said to the fast food clerk who goofed up my order. It may be possible to fall asleep while your brain is stuck in overdrive, but I haven't figured out how.

Of course, since the world is run by you morning people, I struggle. School starts at a woefully early hour, and it doesn't help that I move much more slowly than normal in the AM. So do the boys. We crawl along at a snail's pace, while the clock ticks merrily along.

Forget being cheerful - night owls might be civil when they first get up, and that in itself is a major effort. Cheerful is way beyond our abilities for at least the first half hour. Part of that is we are spending vast amounts of energy yawning and blinking, trying to jump start bodies that are drawn back to our comfortable beds like iron to a magnet.

So please, morning people, show a little compassion. Tone down the cheeriness til we have been conscious a bit. Be tolerant of our slowness during the AM. Don't hold us to major decisions before our first cup of coffee. Oh, and one more thing - five more minutes, please?

THE BEAR WENT OVER THE HAMMOCK

So, it's sometime after one in the morning on Tuesday, and I can't sleep. I decide to check my phone (I was expecting an email) while I was up.

The first thing I see is a text from my honorary son Paul, asking, "Are you still up?"

Given the hour, I was a little concerned, so I shot back, "Are you okay?"

His next text simply said, "Call me."

No parent wants to get a message to call their child at that hour. Imagining car wrecks and other disasters I phoned him.

Paul tells me that he came by the house late to pick up some clean clothes (he does laundry at our place). When he got to our house, he was surprised (and alarmed) to see an adult black bear rooting through our trash.

Okay. Of all the things I was thinking, that wasn't one of them.

Paul and his car apparently scared the bear off, sending it scampering into the woods. Paul broke speed records getting his laundry and then hurried back to the safety of his apartment, when he decided to let me know what had happened.

I woke up Don – I felt as wife this was a "wake your husband" story – and let him know we had trash all over our driveway. Paul further informed us that the evidence showed the bear had been chowing down on some Five Guys fries someone apparently put in our trash can.

That last bit of news was a surprise. I mean, the bear was kind of a surprise, but really shouldn't have been. We live near Highlands Hammock State Park, where black bears live. But seriously, who throws away Five Guys fries?

Don decided, despite the hour, that he should go out and pick up the trash. I was a little nervous about that – what if the bear came back? – but he managed to get things cleaned up without incident. Fortunately, the trash can the county provides wasn't damaged, and things were apparently set to rights.

Then I started wondering if I needed to alert anyone to the fact we'd had a visit from a bear. One of our county commissioners suggested I call the non-emergency number for the sheriff's department and check.

The lady I talked with was very kind but told me there was really no one to report this to. No one had been hurt, so there was nothing that could be done. Oh, and there was a chance the bear could come back since it had found food.

That was unwelcome news. So I am waiting for a call from the company that collects our trash to find out if we can get a bear-proof trash can.

And the fries? A young man living with us confessed to putting the bag of fries in our trash. He's a nice guy and usually intelligent, so we're giving him a pass on throwing away perfectly good fries.

Two remaining thoughts about this incident as I wrap up this column:

First, I found myself craving Five Guys on Tuesday. I indulged in it for dinner, and you can bet I chowed down on fries.

And second, I teach a Ladies Bible Class on Tuesday mornings. We're going through the book of Proverbs. The first verse we considered (and I didn't plan it this way) that morning? Proverbs 17:12. It reads, "Better to meet a bear robbed of her cubs than a fool in his folly."

Coincidence?

I AM STRONG, BUT I AM TIRED

I saw a Facebook meme a while back with this statement: "I am strong, but I am tired." It was something that spoke to me at the time.

It's not just speaking to me today – it is shouting at me at full volume.

I acknowledge I am a strong woman. And I am a blessed woman. I could fill the rest of the column with things I have to be thankful for. Even without spiritual blessings, which are numerous, I have a lot: people who care about me, a roof over my head, more than enough food to eat. Not everyone in the world can lay claim to these blessings, and I am grateful for them.

And while storms – both literal and figurative – have sought to beat me down, in the end I am still standing. I may be trembling with fatigue, but I am standing.

But I am also tired.

I am tired on so many levels. I never seem to get enough sleep lately, even if my Fitbit tells me I've gotten my required eight hours. Even now, late in the morning as I type this out, I want so much to lay back down for just a few minutes.

Intellectually I recognize this as a symptom of the depression I wrestle with, which on occasion still rears its ugly head despite my medication. It doesn't change the fact that I'm tired.

I look about our world and there is much that makes me tired. But it you boiled it all down, it comes to one thing: I'm tired of how we're treating each other.

I watch this a lot on Facebook. People can be cruel when hidden behind a computer screen. They feel safe to spout vile things about others, thinking they themselves can't be touched. They don't realize that what they say speaks volumes about what they are, and it taints them.

And there are the debates. It seems almost anything can become a debate. I even set up a joke debate about what jelly should be paired with peanut butter (by the way, it should be grape) which led to good-natured responses from my friends that I admit brought a smile to my weary face.

Other debates are not so benign. When did agreeing with one's view on something become a test of friendship? I have watched relationships disintegrate because of who someone voted for (or didn't vote for) or what stand they hold on whatever hot button issue the news is playing up this week. What happened to agreeing to disagree?

So, what can I do? I can try to rest when I can. I can try not to sweat the stuff I can't change. And I can try to be the kind of person I wish others were. The Golden Rule – do unto others as you would have them do unto you – isn't just a nice suggestion. It's a command from God.

I know I will get through this. The journey may not be fun, and I will probably need a nap before it's all over, but I will prevail.

And while I may fall down in the process, I know that I can get back up. That is another way to be strong. Even the mightiest among us fall once in a while. They stay mighty by getting back up.

I am strong, but I am tired. But I will see you on the other side of this. I will still be strong, but hopefully less weary than I am now.

Thanks for listening.

A CUT ABOVE

There are some words you never want to hear when sitting in a doctor's office. "Shot" is one. "Enema" is another. And if a doctor ever mentions the phrase "arterial blood gases" to you, that is your signal to either bolt for the nearest exit or be prepared for levels of pain that will have you clinging to the ceiling by your fingernails.

Anyway, a few weeks ago my doctor used another word patients aren't fond of: "surgery."

I was sort of prepared for this news - for weeks we had been going through the medical process of "trying everything but surgery." All of it had been to no avail. So my doctor told me that we had given it "the college try" and it was time to plan for major surgery.

"You'll feel better after this," he assured me.

"Okay," I said, miserable. I would have done almost anything to feel better at that point, maybe even eat liver, or clean my house.

Before I had my surgery, I had to have my "pre-op" appointment. Several things occur during a pre-op appointment:

- They give you all kinds of papers to sign saying you understand what's going to happen to you and all the risks involved. Because of lawsuits, hospitals will list every and any thing that remotely can go wrong during a procedure, including death.

(I remember what the late comedian Lewis Grizzard had to say about such consent forms. He told a nurse that he wanted to take a consent form he had signed in with him during a procedure. When asked why, he replied that if he felt himself dying, he intended to eat the form so they couldn't prove he had signed it.)

– You get at least one needle stuck in you. This is because the hospital can't wait for you to have your surgery to get stuck with a needle. What fun is that? So they make sure you have to have a test of some kind before surgery so they can get blood. At least I got a great blood drawer at Highlands Regional, who can coax blood out of my veins with a minimum of discomfort.

– You get a white plastic bracelet to wear. You are not allowed to remove this bracelet before surgery, no matter what. If you die before the surgery, you will have to be buried with it fastened to your wrist.

Following surgery (which I can give no details on because I thankfully slept through it) I was established on the second floor of Highlands and came under the care of, in my opinion, some of the best nurses on the planet. You want good nurses if you are going to spend any time in a hospital; they can make your stay, if not enjoyable, at least bearable. Plus, while you might see your doctor ten minutes a day while in the hospital, you will spend a lot more time with your nurses.

The nurses who took care of me were fantastic. They made sure I had plenty of ice water. They patiently explained to me that pain medication was NOT my enemy and not taking enough was just making my life more uncomfortable than it needed to be. One stayed nearby when I shakily took my first shower. When I graduated to soft food they tried to find me chocolate pudding. When they couldn't find it they brought me some of the best orange sherbet I've ever eaten. They always smiled at me when I walked up to the nurse's station, which I did a number of times because a) walking was considered good for me and b) the room got boring every once in a while. Once, when I burst into tears for absolutely no apparent reason, a nurse declared, "You need a hug," and gave me one.

I'm home now, slowly recovering from my experience. I honestly would not want to be a patient again any time soon. But if I had to be, I hope I get those nurses again. They are a cut above.

THE FURTHER ADVENTURES OF MY HEART

There is no question that awful things are going on in our country right now. If 2020 were a computer operating system, it would be Windows 95. I, like many others, wish we could somehow reset the thing and try again.

But today I want to talk about something a little closer to home. A tale that will hopefully make you smile a little and even chuckle. The tale of my heart.

Readers of this column may recall that I underwent a stress test not too long ago, to see if I was having any cardiac issues. I fully expected things to come out normal – that's the way these things generally work in my life.

When I scheduled the appointment, my cardiologist Dr. Parnassa said, "I don't want to jinx you, but I think you're going to need a cath."

Well, while I don't want to ascribe magical powers to my doctor, his jinx took hold. To make a long story short, I flunked my stress test. It showed a possible abnormality.

This meant I got to experience the next trip on the cardiac road – a cardiac catherization. This is where the doctor goes into an artery and threads a wire through it until it reaches the coronary arteries.

They then inject dye to see if your passages are clear and the heart is behaving itself.

If there's a problem, say a blockage for example, they might be able to fix it then and there by clearing it out. If there are a lot of problems, then things are a bit more serious.

Don and I both figured that the problem was minor. Still, it had to be addressed. So bright and too early one morning Don and I made our way to Highlands Regional Medical Center so the doctor could stick a hole in me to check out my heart.

The day before, I asked for prayers and good thoughts on Facebook. Now I admit Facebook is not always a positive place to spend time in. But I was given an outpouring of love and goodness from people who saw the post. It touched me deeply, and still does.

Traditionally, caths have been done through an artery in the groin. But my doctor elected to go into an artery in my right wrist. I was okay with that, even knowing there would be restrictions on using that hand for a few days (I'm left-handed). The recovery promised to be quicker, which was also a point in its favor.

To be honest, even though I was apprehensive, the procedure itself wasn't that big a deal. The worst thing about it had nothing to do with the actual cath – the poor woman who tried to start an IV on me had to stick me twice. She apologized profusely the whole time while I gritted my teeth and said it was okay.

During the procedure they gave me enough sedation to feel distant from the whole thing but not enough to knock me out. So I remember being told to turn my head a couple of times. I felt nothing aside from an initial shot to numb my wrist, and I was more than fine with that.

And the result? They found...nothing. No blockage. Nothing amiss. Whatever caused the chest pain that started this whole adventure, my heart was off the hook.

I spent the next couple of days realizing how much I use my right hand when I couldn't (my wrist was splinted so I wouldn't move it and start bleeding all over the place). Even now, while it's much better, I find a lot of typing causes a twinge or two. The doctor says that will go away.

Yes, 2020 is shaping up to be an awful year. And we don't know when (or if) it's going to get any better.

But also in 2020 I learned to appreciate how many people care about me and that my heart, despite my bad habits, is healthy. Somewhere that has to count for something.

UPS AND DOWNS

Sometimes, this column business is easy peasy. I have a great topic I can go on about for the required word length and I get it written and done in plenty of time to make my deadline, no doubt to the delight of the newspaper.

Then there are the times where it's harder. When the topics run away and go into hiding. When nothing seems appropriate or would cause a war I don't want to start.

This is one of those times.

Part of it is that Wednesday found me in a dark place. I strive to be a positive person. After all, as a Christian there's a lot to be positive about. But recent events put me in a depressing place.

This was the week partisanship rose its ugly head in the impeachment hearings and the State of the Union. I saw both the president and the Speaker of the House act like two-year-olds Tuesday night, and that may be unkind to two-year-olds.

And impeachment – where do I begin? Both sides let themselves be controlled by partisanship, rather than what is best for the country. It was a forgone conclusion that Trump would be impeached but not convicted, and it was more because of which party ruled the House and the Senate than any facts.

Then there's the fact that I have friends on both ends of the political spectrum and get hit on both sides with differing opinions. My friends have a right to their opinions and even voicing them. But I've seriously considered hiding certain posts because the name calling is so vicious and the lack of wanting to get along so obvious it's painful to read.

So, when I went to pick up Paul, my honorary son, from work last night I wasn't in the best of moods. He picked up on it and pulled the reason out of me.

He had a ready solution: Dairy Queen. He insisted we go through the drive-thru and get something with chocolate in it for me. While the problem is bigger than even chocolate, I must admit it didn't hurt. Probably because of the love behind it.

Then I posted on Facebook that I was struggling to be positive, and could I get cute pet pics and positive thoughts? I was rewarded with several adorable pictures and encouragement. They also helped. I have good friends who will step in when I cry out.

A quick phone call to my youngest son James brought me advice and the reminder that it's okay to be concerned about what's going on.

Then this morning I self-medicated not with chocolate, but with a video call to my daughter-in-law Amanda, who let me spend time looking at my handsome 7-week-old grandson and interacting with my beloved 22-month-old granddaughter. For my recent birthday, John and Amanda gifted me with a mug that says, "My blessings call me Grandma." How true that is.

And two people who read my post contacted me to make sure I was okay. One of them is my BFF, who is a great sounding board and helpful when I need someone to talk me off a proverbial ledge.

The darkness is still there. Our country's politics are a mess on the moment. I just saw a post on Facebook that is part of the problem – someone who blamed the side he disagreed with for all the problems we have. It's not productive, and it's not going to end it seems.

But the light of friends and family can pierce the darkness and help. A lot. And I am grateful for those who are there for me when I need them.

A LESSON IN PATIENCE

So over a year ago I got wind that the publishers of *Chicken Soup for the Soul* was looking for contributors.

Chicken Soup for the Soul is a book series that's about 23 years old. While they have morphed into other products over the years (including, believe it or not, pet food), you probably know them primarily for their books. The books (they number over 250 by now) contain inspiring stories by people from all walks of life.

Checking things out, I learned that the series was planning a book titled "Random Acts of Kindness." They were looking for inspiring stories where one did an act of kindness or received one.

It didn't take me long to come up with an idea. Years ago, I was the recipient of a major random act of kindness I still recall to this day. I even wrote a column about it soon after it occurred.

So, using the column to refresh my memory (yes, I still have copies of my old columns) I wrote about that hot day in Sebring when a stranger touched my life. I emailed the essay to the editors at *Chicken Soup,* and waited.

And...nothing happened.

I knew I'd gotten the essay in before the deadline. I also knew (in my head) that things like this could take time.

But weeks turned into months. And still nothing.

It didn't help that a friend of mine, who'd submitted to another book for *Chicken Soup*, got accepted relatively quickly. Don't get me wrong, I was happy for her. It was great news for her. But I have to admit there was a twinge of..."what about me?"

More months went by. I did the best I could to put the whole thing out of my mind. Writers hear "no" a lot more often than they hear "yes." I had other fish to fry. It wasn't like I didn't have sales elsewhere.

But...this was *Chicken Soup for the Soul*. For me, personally, a big deal. It was a chance to be in a series that a lot of people read. A series that touched a lot of lives.

I wanted to be a part of that.

The one year mark came and went. I still thought of that little essay from time to time, but was at the point I could shrug and move on. I think in some circles that's called "acceptance."

And then, November 5th, 2016, I received the following email from D'ette Corona, Associate Publisher for *Chicken Soup for the Soul*:

"Dear Laura: Your story 'Touched by an Angel' has made it to the final selection round for *Chicken Soup for the Soul: Random Acts of Kindness...*"

There was more – like there was no guarantee I'd be selected finally but just in case, would I fill out a form? I filled out the form without hesitation. Hope was alive again.

This time the wait was a few weeks. I got another email asking me to check on edits of my essay, that had made it to the final round. It wasn't quite a confirmation yet, but a good sign.

Then, December 13th, I got an early Christmas present – an email confirming that my little essay, written over a year ago, was going to appear in *Chicken Soup for the Soul: Random Acts of Kindness*, scheduled to come out February 7th, 2017.

If you check your calendar, that was yesterday. The book is available now. My essay is one of 101 stories of kindness. Worth a read, especially if you're feeling low.

It goes to show that sometimes, good things happen if you are just patient enough. I know they did for me.

CAN FAT BE USEFUL?

This is a tough time of year if, like me, you're supposed to be losing weight. I mean, it's never easy to lose weight as far as I'm concerned, but this time of year is (if you'll pardon the phrase) no picnic.

Think about it. Start with Thanksgiving, which was not created with dieters in mind. You have stuffing, you have mashed potatoes, you have cranberry sauce...you have me drooling while I type this... (and we haven't even gotten to pie).

Then the time between Thanksgiving and Christmas? You have cookies, cake, candy, possibly more pie. If you go to parties or gatherings there's all kinds of goodies. Most of them have enough calories in them to sink a battleship and toast any diet you might be on.

I know I've fallen off the diet wagon. Hard. I'm avoiding my scale as much as possible for the moment and praying Don won't ask me how the whole weight loss thing is going. (He probably will when he reads this column. This will not be an enjoyable conversation).

The thing is, I have eyes. They work well enough to tell me I'm overweight when I look in the mirror. I see the fat on me. I know it's not good for me to have it.

But I like to eat. And it's not like I can give up food, at least not for a long period of time.

People will say that of course you have to eat, you just have to choose to eat the right things. As in, things that you obviously aren't eating right now because if you were you wouldn't have all that fat on you. Right?

Look, I'd be a lot more willing to diet if we could get the tastes right. Why can't broccoli taste like mashed potatoes? Salad taste like grilled cheese? Brussels sprouts taste like anything else?

If you, like me, are carting around a few extra pounds, you might find this recent news story of interest. Apparently, two women found a use for their extra poundage – they used it to assist in an attempt at shoplifting.

I am not kidding. According to Edmond, Oklahoma police Ailene Brown and Shmeco Thomas tried to make off with about $2600 worth of store merchandise by stuffing it under their breasts and their belly fat.

According to one officer, "These two were actually concealing them in areas of their body where excess skin was, under their chest area and armpits."

The list of items include four pairs of boots, three pairs of jeans, a pair of gloves and a wallet.

The items made me think. I could probably conceal a pair of gloves or a wallet under certain large portions of my anatomy. Three pairs of jeans? That's tough. And boots? I haven't seen a picture of the accused and can't speak to how big they are. But surely they'd have to be bigger than me to pull that off.

While I'm not encouraging anyone to shoplift, I think the idea of our fat actually being useful could take the sting out of our poor dietary practices. Maybe someone more creative than I am can come up with some ideas that aren't illegal or immoral.

I'd give more time and thought to this, but my creativity is tied up in how I'm going to explain this column to Don. And how I'm going to avoid that stupid scale until 2011. Wish me luck.

MOM

I had a nice Mother's Day. Both John and James took the time to call me, Don gave me flowers and a lovely card, and it was overall a good day. But there was a touch of the bittersweet to it: for some reason, my thoughts kept going back to my mom, who left this earth too young 19 years ago.

She was born in Brooklyn, New York in 1929, and was a Brooklyn girl through and through. We used to joke that the city would never die as long as my mom was around – even years in Florida couldn't get rid of the tang of Brooklyn in her voice.

Mom didn't finish high school, due to family obligations. She had three daughters and a son and watched them go through school. When my brother was finishing up his journey through public education, Mom decided it was time she finished her own schooling. She got her GED and then went on to become an LPN. My siblings and I were so proud of her for doing all that.

Mom was the one who gifted me with a love of reading and words in general. In fact, I give her credit in part for my becoming a writer. I regret that she didn't live to see me go into fiction writing – I would have loved her input on my novels and stories.

One other thing she gave me was compassion for young people.

Mom liked our friends and was a willing shoulder and ear to those who were having problems. Whenever Don and I have reached out to a young person to help them out, I like to think I'm honoring her in a small way.

She was brash and sassy and didn't take a lot of garbage from others. It was entertaining to listen to her deal with a phone solicitor – she usually had a snappy comeback that I'm sure made them regret calling our house.

Mom had her quirks. She never learned how to drive. Her excuse was that she was afraid she'd try to arrest other drivers who misbehaved on the road. She'd also joked that New York refused to give her a license simply because she couldn't stop, back up, or turn. I never learned the rest of the story, and we as a family worked around the fact she didn't drive.

A lifelong diehard Republican, Mom had strong opinions concerning politics. I've wondered what she'd make of the current mess we have in Washington, DC. I can almost hear her bemoaning the nastiness that politics have become, and while I don't know how she would've voted in 2016, I'm pretty sure it wouldn't have been for Hillary.

Another bad habit she had that I wish with all my heart she could've stopped was smoking. She started young, and never managed to quit, despite knowing the risks. Over time she developed breast cancer and quit briefly, but then went back to the cigarettes. Even being on oxygen 24/7 and getting lung cancer didn't make her quit – she smoked until the day she died.

I miss my mom. I miss talking to her, debating with her, playing word games with her. If you're lucky enough to still have your mom alive, you have a blessing. Give her a call, or if it's feasible, go by and see her, just to give her a hug. Right now, I wish I could.

TO CLEAN OR NOT TO CLEAN

I am the first one to admit that when God gave out motivation to clean a house, I was off somewhere reading. In my house, I'm lucky to keep the way to the exits clear.

Part of the problem is clutter. My office, for example, needs someone to assist me in getting rid of stuff that I have no good reason to hang on to but do so anyway. There's also a bunch of magazines under a computer table I should either skim or admit I'm never going to look at and throw away.

In the house, the kitchen is probably in the best shape, and that's not all my doing. Mike, a young man living with us at the moment, loves to cook and has decided the kitchen is his project. Thanks to him and some help from me, things are more or less neat.

But there are reasons my house is in a state of disarray. It's not just that housework isn't one of my favorite activities. There are extenuating circumstances that are at work here. Let me list a few:

Books. I am a firm believer in the saying, "The problem isn't too many books, it's not enough shelf space." We have books in nearly every room of the house. Our current shelf space is not able to contain them all, so they've found themselves in various other spots.

Yes, I have a Kindle. But that doesn't mean I don't love and occasionally get my hands on print books. They have their place in my home.

What's that you say? Get rid of some of them? Just the thought of that makes my palms sweaty. These are my friends. How do you get rid of friends?

Dog. Gerry is Paul's dog, but for now lives with us. Gerry is half Corgi, half Jack Russell terrier, and all dog. Like any dog, he sheds. Which means there is fur everywhere. Yes, even on the furniture because we do let him on it. Hey, he lives here.

This means I quickly fill my vacuum's canister with fur when I do the floors. It's a small price to pay for someone so cute. But it does add to the struggle.

Time. This was more of a problem when my mother-in-law was alive. When I was a full-time caregiver, there wasn't time or energy to tackle the house. I did the minimum to keep things functioning and hoped people would understand.

While this is less of a problem now, it's still there. As I try to be a full-time writer the time must come from somewhere. And most of the time, given the choice between cleaning the house and creating fiction, the latter is more fun. I say "most of the time" because house-work can be a delaying tactic when the writing is going badly. True story.

Bad habits. I know I have developed bad habits of not cleaning over the years. I used to be much better at it than I am. I know I should do better and that there are all kinds of methods out there to help me improve. I just need to take a deep breath and make it a priority.

I probably will never be confused with Suzy Homemaker. But hopefully I can overcome some of these issues and have a cleaner house to show for it. Until then, please be kind if you come visit. And don't wear a white glove.

THE JOURNEY TO A PHOTO

Those of you who read my column in the Highlands News-Sun will see something different today. For the first time in a number of years, there will be a photo to go with the column.

Usually, columns like mine display a photo of the columnist. This is something that I have resisted for many years. Why? What's the big deal?

The thing is, I am one of those people who don't like having their picture taken. I look in the mirror and don't like what I see. To be blunt, I don't think I'm attractive.

This is a struggle. I am overweight. Though they have faded over the years, I still bear scars from bouts of acne as a teenager. My face isn't exactly the one you see on models.

So I really didn't want a picture for the column. Romona Washington, a wise woman, didn't push the issue. She simply waited me out.

And I slowly came to the conclusion that this was something I needed to do. I have written this column for nearly 25 years. It was time to let people see me.

I informed Romona of my intentions, and her enthusiastic "Finally!" told me I might have been a wee bit stubborn about the thing. But I was now committed to getting a picture made.

I found a photographer, Angel M. Huergo. Her reviews were positive and indicated she was good with nervous people. That's me. Nervous person. So I contacted her and made arrangements for a photo shoot.

I talked to friends about my issue. Not one person told me, "You're right; you're unattractive." Instead, they offered support and encouragement, urging me to get my hair and makeup done for the shoot.

They also pointed out that this was a good thing I was doing, not just for me, but for those like me, who feel we must be invisible because we don't measure up to some standard of beauty. They told me I deserved to be seen.

So the day of the shoot I did so. I kept a wary eye on the weather that day – we were taking pictures outdoors and if it rained we'd have to postpone. Thankfully, though it rained before and after, the time of our shoot was dry.

Angel was marvelous. She put me at ease and took a bunch of pictures. I took the advice of one of my friends and when she told me to smile I thought about my grandbabies. That made it easy to smile.

Yesterday I got the pictures. I'd love to tell you that looking them over was easy, but it wasn't. Not that Angel did a bad job. She was worth every penny.

The issue was looking at these photos and accepting – even approving – of the woman they showed.

There is a tension between accepting and liking who you are at a given moment and recognizing there are things you want to change. Both can happen at the same time, I'm told.

I want to lose weight. But even if I do I will never be skinny – my days of weighing 115 pounds are in the past. I will probably always have a little padding.

Can I accept my overweight self, understanding she is who I am at the moment, and she deserves love and respect, just like anyone else? Especially from me?

Putting a picture with this column is a step towards that. I have decided to move out of my comfort zone and let you see me.

See me. See all of me.

Ready or not, here I am..

TRAVEL

Don and I enjoy traveling, and our trips often make it into my column in some form or fashion. Some of these are about the destinations, others are about the journey. Almost all of them have something amusing about them, because those kinds of things happen when I travel.
There's also a column about flying shortly after 9/11, which seems so far away now that I look back at it. That is a more serious look at travel and was a prelude to what airline travel would become after twenty-two years. So turn the page and take some trips with me.

SNOW, ICE, AND NORTHERN LIGHTS

W here do I start to talk about the last ten days in Norway? Perhaps with the Northern Lights. We got a glimpse of them one night while on our cruise ship. Lucky for us, the best view was on the deck we were staying on and our cabin was near the doors to the outside. So we got a good look at them.

It is hard to describe seeing the Northern Lights for real rather than in pictures. They were dimmer than I expected, a soft green light that moved across the sky. It was a beautiful sight to see. Trust me, it was well worth standing outside in a wind so frigid my face froze.

Unfortunately, that night was our one look at them. You need clear skies to view the lights, and the weather decided it wasn't going to cooperate with us after that night. In fact, there were onshore excursions that were cancelled due to weather. Our last two days at sea had the large ship rocking some, which was soothing if you were laying in bed but made walking an adventure.

I do not blame the cruise line for any of this. Good as they were in their treatment of us, they could not control the weather. Instead they worked hard to make sure we enjoyed ourselves and were comfortable.

They made extra sure we ate. If you've ever been on a cruise ship you know that one of the primary forms of entertainment is eating. Breakfast and lunch were buffets while dinner was an excellent three course meal. While I didn't get to try everything offered (if I had the numbers on the scale would be a lot scarier than they are at the moment) I did sample a few things I don't recall eating before, such as ox and stewed reindeer. Yes, I ate reindeer meat. Don't tell Rudolph.

Don and I got to visit a number of Norwegian coastal towns while on the cruise. This is where my husband's research and preparation for the trip really shone. Thanks to him we didn't freeze to death on any of these excursions – in fact, we were so comfortable we didn't have to use some of the things we'd brought such as stuff called "Hot Hands," which from the description on the packaging is like sticking a mini-heater in your pocket.

One item we did use extensively is something called – I am not kidding – "Yaktrax." Yaktrax are essentially chains you can strap to the bottom of your boots or shoes to keep your footing on ice and snow.

I can testify that these babies work. I could feel them gripping the ice when I put my foot down. This did not keep me from hanging on to Don's arm – a Norwegian toddler is more surefooted than I am when it comes to walking on snow and ice. But without these on my boots I am sure there would have been several times I'd have wound up flat on my back or my rear, which would have entertained anyone watching while I would be wondering if one could really die of embarrassment.

Sadly, only one of my Yaktrax made it home. The other one slipped off my boot somewhere when we traveled from Kirkenes to our hotel in Oslo. Which is a shame because if I ever go anyplace there's a chance of snow and ice I want to have these handy.

I will be candid. I would not choose to live in Norway. It is cold. Eating out costs a small fortune. I'm not sure they've heard of Diet Dr. Pepper.

But I'm not opposed to visiting the place again. It is a beautiful country, and the people are kind and friendly. And the lights are still there. I wouldn't mind finding them just one more time.

HUNTING THE LIGHTS

I'm typing this sitting in a very nice hotel room in Tromso, Norway. I've been here since the 29th and will remain here a few more days before winging my way back to sunny warm Florida.

Getting here was an adventure in and of itself. Someone forgot to notify us that our flight to Newark was leaving early, thus we arrived at the gate too late to board. Then the next plane we got on headed for Newark developed engine trouble – fortunately while we were still on the ground. We were then switched to yet another airplane and finally got to Newark still having plenty of time to catch our evening flight to Oslo. Things were fairly routine from there.

Why am I here? Why did I endure hours of travel, four airports, and a six hour time change? Why did I come to a place where the sun doesn't even peek over the horizon and pale sunlight is available for about four hours a day? Where the temperatures are frigid by Floridian standards? Maybe by anyone's standards?

Two words: Northern Lights.

When we were in Norway last January, we only got a brief glimpse of the lights one night. Due to our inexperience, we didn't take any pictures worth sharing. It was a small disappointment in what was overall a wonderful trip.

But Don and I are fascinated by the lights. We have pictures of them hanging on our walls. We really wanted a good look at them.

So we decided to come back with the goal of hunting down the beautiful but sometimes elusive Northern Lights.

We've been out twice so far. Both times with a tour group called Northern Shots (www.northernshotstours.com). We will go out with another tour company later this week. But so far our experience has been with this group.

I have to say Don and I were very pleased with Northern Shots. The first night we were in a small group of eight, which meant lots of personal attention. The second night was a much larger group, but the tour guide was very kind and helpful to us, especially when it came to getting to the place where we found the lights.

You see, you have to drive away from the city to see the lights and go someplace dark. Our guides took us near a beach off an island about an hour and a half out of town. Then you had to climb up a small hill and down again to get to the perfect spot. A hill covered in rocks, snow, and ice.

Those of you who know me will recognize there is some trouble with this. I am not surefooted on a flat surface, much less a bumpy, icy one. It took Don and the guide to get me up and down these hills. I managed to keep falling to a minimum and have survived the experience thus far with only a slightly skinned knee.

But the cold, the knee, the travelling – it was all worth it for the sights we saw.

The Northern lights shimmered and spread across the sky. You might think they were light passing through clouds, except there was no light source and no clouds. They were bright and they were beautiful.

More camera savvy this time, we have gotten fantastic pictures that we will share on Facebook. Pictures intensify the colors – the lights are much paler to the naked eye. But seeing them is an experience to store up and treasure.

Yes, I'm glad I came back to hunt the lights. It's been a dream of

Don's and mine for a while. And it's always nice to have a dream come true.

Even if it means climbing an icy hill or two.

ADVENTURES IN TRAVELING

This Thanksgiving, as has become our tradition, Don and I travelled to South Carolina to visit our oldest son John, his wife Amanda, and our two adorable grandbabies, Lavinia and Matthias.

It was a wonderful visit with family. Our younger son James and his girlfriend Mary also showed up, and we had a lot of time to eat, play board games, and talk.

Amanda and John are gracious hosts. They put up with the disruption our visits cause with grace and patience. In return we love on our grandbabies and even babysit them if Mommy and Daddy want some alone time.

Getting to South Carolina was okay, even though we were routed through Atlanta (I think when you die, you may get to your ultimate destination via Atlanta, but I can't prove this). But getting back was a little less straightforward.

First off, we had to leave the house at four in the morning to get to the airport for a 5:55 am flight. We loaded our things into John's car, and I stuck my phone in my jacket pocket.

When we got to the airport, we unloaded, hugged goodbye and

John pulled away. At that point, I realized my phone was no longer in my possession. It had fallen out in the car.

Don immediately tried to call John's phone, which went to voicemail. I then asked for my husband's phone and dialed my number.

"Well, this is interesting," my son said when he answered my phone. I asked him to please come back to the airport and he was gracious enough to do so and hand over my device, which did NOT go back in the jacket pocket.

Security looked like it would be quick – Greenville International Airport is small and there weren't a lot of people there. They let us leave our electronics in our backpacks and I sent my stuff through the scanner.

They pulled my bag aside. This didn't concern me very much – In addition to my laptop, I had an iPad, a Kindle, and a Nintendo Switch in the bag. I figured they just needed to look them over.

They didn't like something about my laptop. They decided to rescan it, and I began to get nervous. What if they confiscated it? This is not just my travel laptop, it has my writing stuff on it, as well as other things I'd rather not lose.

Poor Don, who'd gotten through security with no hassle, kept looking over at me wondering what was going on. I didn't want to leave my stuff, so I stood there in stocking feet and waited to be cleared.

Finally, they decided the laptop was okay and let me have it and the rest of my gear back.

When we got to Atlanta, the airline decided to toss me a monkey wrench. When I fly, I wear a waist pack to carry my wallet and other small items. 99% of the time, this is acceptable and not counted towards the two bag limit airlines have concerning carry ons.

This time they busted me. The announced that waist packs counted as a carryon and passengers wearing them either had to consolidate into two items or check a bag.

I admit it made me cranky. I emptied the contents of the waist pack into my backpack and stuffed the waist pack itself inside as well. Fortunately, it all fit. Checking a bag was a non-starter because I refuse to check my backpack (not only does it carry my electronics, but also my medication) and the airlines aren't crazy about checking a bag with a CPAP in it.

Despite all that we arrived alive back in Florida and got home at a decent hour.

I hope any holiday travel plans you have go smoothly this season. Just remember to leave time to get through security and if you have a waist pack, make sure your other carry on has room for your stuff. Just in case.

A TRIP TO NEW YORK CITY

So one of the things on Don's and my list of trips we wanted to take was New York City. Why, you may ask, that particular place? For Don it was someplace he'd never been and was curious about. As for me, though I was born in Brooklyn and even traveled to New York City from time to time my family never did all the "tourist" things that you'd expect us to.

It was a trip we talked about often but kept putting off for various reasons. Life kept throwing us curve balls. We have obligations. How could we pull this off?

Finally, this past summer, Don was done with putting it off. "We're going to New York City in October," he told me.

My first thought was my mother-in-law. She needs a lot of care. While we'd managed to pull off a few days in Orlando by arranging for her care, New York City was a different matter. We'd be gone a day longer and we wouldn't be just 2 hours away if something went wrong.

So I asked, "What about Mom?"

"We'll figure something out," said my confident husband.

I had reservations, but the trip was tempting. 5 days, just me and

Don on a vacation. By ourselves (we had others with us in Orlando). Downtime that if I were honest with myself I badly needed.

So we made plans. We found a cheerful and enthusiastic nurse who was willing to come in part of the time to help us out. Others were recruited to lend a hand for the rest of the time. I did my part, arranging for someone to take my Wednesday night Bible class, updating my list of Mom's medications and in general trying to keep the worry at bay.

Today rolled around bright and early. The nurse arrived and shooed us away, telling us not to worry and to have a good time. We headed for Orlando and the airport there, grateful that Hurricane Michael wasn't barreling across the state at the moment, though I really wish he'd left the people in the panhandle alone.

Our travel plans benefitted from the welcome news that we had gotten TSA/pre-approval on our tickets, so security at the airport was pretty painless. Our flight wound up leaving on time and before I could fret too much we were landing at JFK Airport.

While I'd downloaded the Uber app, I hadn't used it before so Don and I decided to simply grab a taxi from the airport to our hotel. After a brief wait in line we were handed over to a man whose name I forget and whose speech makes me suspect that English isn't his native tongue. He loaded our luggage in the back, got us seated, and we took off.

Within minutes I was grateful that we'd decided to forgo renting a car for this trip. New York driving makes U. S. 27 look like a leisurely stroll in a park. I kept my mouth shut and tried to concentrate on the scenery and my phone instead of the traffic. Our driver mostly ignored us, occasionally muttering in a foreign language. I hope it wasn't about us.

We arrived at the Hotel Edison, a hotel in Times Square that was recommended to us. It's nice enough, though the room is smaller than we're used to. But it has a Keurig in it, as well as other necessities, so I think we'll be just fine.

After unloading, we treated ourselves to pizza at a place called John's Pizzeria. If you ever go to New York City, you have to try this place. We got a garlic, ham, and mushroom pizza and it tasted fresh and delicious. We'll need to do a lot of walking after that meal, but I think that's going to happen.

But it's only the first day, and I'm out of room for the column anyway. More on the trip next week. See you then.

NEW YORK, NEW YORK

I t is impossible to condense my five days in New York City to 600 words.

I blame the designers of the city in part. I can't prove this, but I suspect that anyone designing anything in New York City was told "go big or go home." And they all took it to heart.

Take Times Square, where Don and I stayed. Imagine being surrounded by tall buildings that have gigantic electronic billboards flashing all kinds of advertisements and information. And this goes on for blocks and blocks. Think of never-ending traffic and swarms of people on the street, some intent on parting you with your money.

I don't mean that last in the sense we were pickpocketed or anything like that. Despite what you may have heard about the Big Apple, we didn't encounter any criminal activity while we were there. We WERE taken advantage of once, which I share with you as a cautionary tale lest you venture into the big city yourself.

While we walked about Times Square, we encountered some people dresses up as popular Marvel characters. I wanted a picture of one, and one of them helpfully put us in a group photo and took the picture for us.

Once it was done, we were informed we were required to tip

everyone involved – including the guy who took the picture with OUR camera. And we're not talking a couple of dollars here. We paid and privately agreed not to get our pictures taken with anyone the rest of the trip.

But as fascinating as Times Square is, we didn't spend our whole trip there (though we could've spent the whole trip attending Broadway shows in and around Times Square). On the advice of a friend, we paid a visit to the Metropolitan Museum of Art. This meant braving the New York Subway system, which made me a little nervous.

Besides the fact there are way too many stairs and you couldn't always make out what the conductor was saying, the subway system isn't too bad. I'd heard stories about rats and filth, but I saw no vermin in our travels and from my perspective the subway was relatively clean. It was cheap and got us where we needed to go. They even have an app for your phone that proved invaluable in planning our routes.

Back to the museum. This building is three city blocks long and several stories high. This was another place we could've spent the entire trip and maybe still not seen all of it. As it was, we saw a small portion of the museum, which had a lot of sculpture. Picture taking was allowed, and we snapped away.

Then there was the Statue of Liberty. We decided to forgo a trip to the crown of the statue, which is a strenuous climb of 352 steps. We did go up into the pedestal, which has a convenient elevator. Here again, we found we didn't have time for everything – we had to forgo a trip to nearby Ellis Island because we spent so much time at the statue. But it was worth it. Lady Liberty is awesome in person.

We did other things as well, but I am rapidly running out of room in this column. One thing I want to add was we walked a lot – even taking the subway required some shoe leather to get where we needed to go – and somewhere, somehow, I managed to mildly sprain or strain my ankle. Fortunately, this didn't become an issue until the day we left, when it was quite painful and we had to get a wheelchair to get through the airport. Not a souvenir I wanted to add to all we bought, but oh well.

All in all, a successful trip, even if it was too short. We plan to return at some point to see the things we missed. Maybe this time I can skip the sprained ankle.

A TRIP TO OHIO

Last weekend found me in Cleveland, Ohio. It was not for business. I was visiting my youngest son James and his wife Ali, who I hadn't seen in too many months.

This meant braving the friendly skies and airport security. While I got through security unscathed and the trip to Cleveland was uneventful, something rather unsettling happened at the end of the flight.

There I was, standing in the aisle, with my trusty backpack and roll-on carryon, waiting in line to get off the plane. A flight attendant stopped us as some of us neared the door and asked us to wait. She said (I am not kidding) that there were too many bags at the rear of the plane and they were concerned that the front of the thing would tip up.

This is NOT what you want to tell someone with balance issues. I eyed the seat next to me, wondering if I could slip into it fast if I felt the plane start to tip. After a few uneasy moments, they allowed us to get off the airplane and I breathed a sigh of relief. No tipping up today!

James came to get me after work, and promptly took me to see Lake Erie. I've never seen any of the Great Lakes before, so this was a treat. The thing is HUGE. It had small waves lapping a sandy shore. You could almost trick yourself into thinking you were on a beach somewhere, except the water wasn't salty.

Along with seeing James and Ali, I got to spend time with their lovable dog Hobbes. Hobbes, who may be part Labrador (I don't remember), is big and goofy and in spite of the time apart seemed to remember me. James and Ali also have a cat, but the cat made it clear it wanted nothing to do with me. Oh well.

I have to say up front that James and Ali made it their business to spoil me rotten from the time I got there until I left. I also suspect that James was subtly trying to convince me that Cleveland was a great place to live, didn't I want to come up permanently?

I have to say my son is aware of what might draw me. Friday he took me to two of Cleveland's libraries. One of them made me think of Sebring's. The other...

Ah, yes, the other. It is located near James' apartment and is large and airy. It not only has books galore, but a garden to sit and read in and – I am not kidding – 3D printers patrons can use. 3D!

It's a library to happily get lost in. James could have left me there in the morning and picked me up at dinnertime and I wouldn't have been bored. He didn't, of course – after all, I'd come to visit him, not the library – but it's a thought for next time.

And it made me miss the times I'd linger at our local libraries. I'd forgotten what a haven they were. I'm planning to go back more regularly, so thank Cleveland for reminding me of what a treasure a library is.

I had fun the all too few days I spent in Cleveland. A friend told me its nickname is "The Mistake on the Lake," but I think that's rather unfair. It's a nice place to live and seems to be taking good care of my son and his wife, so I'm happy with it.

As long as James and Ali are there, I will find a reason to go back to Cleveland. And maybe spend more time in that library. But don't worry, I'll be back. There's no place like home.

WILD WONDERFUL ALASKA

I t seemed like a good idea at the time. Take a vacation to Alaska, a place we had never been, where temperatures in the 90's were unheard of. It would be fun. It would be an adventure! In our planning, we forgot the old saying, "be careful what you wish for."

Our first clue that things might be a little more exciting than we bargained for occurred on the flight into Anchorage. Warning number one: it is a LONG flight to Alaska. Throw in the fact that the airlines are constantly trying to reduce such luxuries as leg room on their flights and you have a new method of aggravating people.

To top it off, the landing was more exciting than anyone who isn't a teenage boy would want. I am nervous about landing anyway, but this time we hit some wind while just over the runway. The plane tilted, and there was a general cry of alarm.

Of course, since you are reading this column, we landed safely, but it was a scary few seconds.

We were fortunate in that we started our stay in Anchorage in a nice hotel downtown. The niceness of it was lost on us early one morning when the fire alarm went off. We quickly determined that a 12th floor room was not the best place to be when a fire alarm goes off because that means descending 12 flights of stairs. Throw in being half awake and no coffee and you will understand I was not quite so enthusiastic about the vacation by the time I stumbled outside.

Weather was to blame for two other unscheduled thrills during our stay. We had signed up for a day cruise to see Alaskan wildlife and glaciers. Several hours into the trip, it had to be cut short due to 8 to 10 foot waves in our route. By the time the decision was made, the smaller waves were enough for my stomach to want to go back anyway.

We managed to miss the next "adventure" - heavy rains had caused a creek to flood near one place we were scheduled to stay at. This caused two cabins in the place to attempt to imitate boats. Fortunately, no one was hurt, and we were referred to another place to stay at.

Of course at this point you might wonder if I had a good time. The answer is a solid yes. You have to balance the mishaps we suffered, which in total amounted to simple inconveniences, with the beauty and fun of Alaska.

In the summer, the sun doesn't set until after midnight. Imagine strolling downtown at 10:30 PM with it still being light outside. We felt pretty safe, as opposed to walking downtown at 10:30 PM most cities in the "lower 48."

Alaska has a lot of wilderness in it - the entire state houses less than 1 million souls. We saw wild sheep grazing on the mountains. Don and James had a close encounter with a moose. We had the experience of snow in July at Denali National Park. We caught a glimpse of a bear in the distance and were taught what to do if we happened upon one (you do not scream and run, which would be my first choice).

We saw bald eagles nesting in the wild and sea lions playing beside our boat. We got close to a glacier. Not close enough to touch, but close enough to see the size of it and understand how ice could transform the land around it.

I would not live in Alaska. The long days in the summer are offset by long nights in the winter, and I doubt I would ever fully adjust to either. The winters are cold and bitter - something I don't miss here in sunny Florida.

But the state is worth another look. Alaska is a great place to visit. Just don't ask me to live there.

TRAVEL TALES

I'm typing this column amid getting ready for a trip. I will be heading to Las Vegas, Nevada, for a week-long writing workshop/conference.

I am both looking forward to the trip and nervous about it. The nerves are because I'm leaving the homestead in the hands of my husband Don, who while a perfectly capable person might not realize something needs to be done because I'm the one who does it all the time.

It's silly, of course. Paul will be helping out, and both of them are mature human beings who can take care of themselves. But I've already come up with a plan for them to text me if they need some question answered. Call it being a mom.

Because I live far away from the airport, I will be driving tomorrow for over two hours. I'm hoping to leave early enough that I don't have to catch lunch at the airport, which tends to be pricey. There's also a Cracker Barrel on the way to the airport, and I'm not one to skip Cracker Barrel if I get a chance for it.

I do not plan to eat in my car. According to a story I read on www.foxnews.com, a Connecticut man apparently got into trouble last

April when a police officer thought he saw him talking on his cell phone while driving, a big no-no in Connecticut.

The driver, Jason Stiber, claims the cop was mistaken – what the officer took to be a phone was really a McDonald's hash brown that he was consuming while driving. The officer apparently didn't buy the story and hit Stiber with a $300 ticket.

Stiber has been fighting the ticket, appealing a ruling he lost previously. John Thygerson, Stiber's attorney, allegedly submitted phone records proving Stiber wasn't on the phone at the time of the event and claims his client is innocent. A ruling is expected by April 5th of this year.

I admit to both eating and talking on the phone while driving (I can sense my best friend wanting to smack me upside the head for that). I don't text and drive – that way lies accidents – but sometimes I need to communicate with someone while on the road. So, I'm glad I live in Florida where it's not against the law – yet.

When I fly to Vegas, I'm hoping for an uneventful trip. I certainly don't want to experience what Moria Boxall, a Scottish woman, endured after a 9,000-mile flight from Australia to Scotland. It seems she brought home a stowaway – a small spotted python that took up residence in one of her shoes.

The article I read on www.cnn.com doesn't indicate how said python got into her suitcase and her shoe. It does say it was starting to shed its skin, which you can see in the pictures that Boxall or some other calm person was able to take.

Me? Finding a snake in my shoe – even a "cute little baby" snake, as a friend of mine referred to it – would result in some shrieking and running. Probably not much picture taking.

Anyway, Boxall did have the presence of mind to call an animal protection organization that took the small non-venomous snake into quarantine in Edinburgh. I have no idea what will happen to it, but I hope they find a comfy shoe for it to live in while they decide.

So, here's to no traffic tickets and no snakes on my trip. And that the house is still standing when I get back. Of course, it will be. Right?

FLYING AFTER 9/11

S everal months ago, Don mentioned a medical convention that would be held in Vermont during the month of October. He dangled several enticements regarding it. No kids (some friends of ours expressed a willingness to watch the boys, proof we have very GOOD friends), colorful leaves, and the Ben and Jerry's Ice Cream factory. I decided it might be fun to go with him on this trip, and we made the requisite airline reservations.

And then came September 11th....

Both of us gave some thoughts to our travel plans following that terrible day. I will not lie - we toyed with the idea of canceling the entire thing. Flying in and of itself already makes me a little nervous. It's not a terrified, armrest-gripping fear most of the time, more of a general unease during takeoff and landings. I've heard that those are the times a problem is most likely to occur, so I figure once we are actually in the air we're pretty safe.

In the end, we decided to go through with our plans and travel to Vermont by air. When friends and family found out about our plans, some of them called us brave. Some no doubt found this as even more evidence that we were crazy. One family member even called and tried to talk us out of traveling. But Don and I both figured the odds were in our favor in this, and what were we going to do? Walk to Vermont?

We were informed that we needed to be at the airport 2 ½ hours early, a time frame my husband took VERY seriously. Alone, I might have tried to fudge it a little, especially since arriving that early would require me to get up horribly early - not my way to start a fun week away from home. But Don got me up, and we staggered to the airport, barely conscious.

For those of you who have been avoiding airports lately, let me explain to you what you are missing:

No sharp items are allowed. None. You can put them in your suitcase, but not in any carry-on bag. This includes nail clippers, small sewing scissors, and razor blades.

You will be asked for a picture ID practically everywhere you go in the airport. Which means way too many people saw my awful driver's license picture. I reckon safety is worth humiliation, but I wish the Department of Motor Vehicles would learn how to take decent photos.

You will see lots of soldiers wearing green camouflage and carrying impressive-looking guns as you pass through security. I would not want to mess with any of these men. I wouldn't even be RUDE to one of these guys. I did thank one of them for being there. It is reassuring to know they are keeping an eye on things.

(By the way, one of my kids asked me if I saw any sky marshals. I must admit I don't know if I did or not. Sky marshals are not in the habit of wearing superhero costumes or big signs proclaiming, "I AM A SKY MARSHAL!")

You may or may not be subject to a random search or two. When we were getting ready to head for our connecting flight out of Newark into Burlington, Don was pulled from the line and "wanded" - that means a metal detecting wand was passed over his body. When I said I was traveling with him, they decided to go ahead and wand me too. I was also made to flip my belt buckle and prove there was nothing behind it. After we proved we were harmless, we were allowed to head for the plane.

On the way back to Florida, Don's briefcase was pulled and searched because they couldn't see everything in it on the x-ray machine. They discovered my husband carries a lot of reading material when he travels. They also discovered the bag weighs a ton - had anyone tried to mess with us on the plane all we would have had to do is whack him in the head with Don's briefcase and the terrorist wouldn't have woke up until two hours after we landed.

When we landed in Newark last week, something interesting happened; there was scattered applause. I think I also heard a few people clap when we landed in Orlando about a week later. I know I heard relief in my sister's voice when I called to tell her we were on the ground and none the worse for wear.

Some things have not changed with the airline industry. The seats still are not designed with normal human beings in mind. The food still does not make your taste buds quiver with delight (I guess I should be thankful we GOT food). Baggage claim is still an adventure. But let me contrast that with one fact - flying is still a relatively safe way to travel. If I have to choose one quality I desire above all with the airlines, that is the one I will certainly pick.

A GRAND CANYON

One thing Don had planned to do while we were on vacation this year was to see the Grand Canyon. I agreed, thinking it would be fun and picturesque. I also liked the fact that we would be ferried over to the canyon by a plane. Little did I know this would be the worst part.

Well, on the day we were scheduled to take our tour, we found ourselves waiting outside our hotel for the bus that would take us to our tour plane. We were standing in what shade we could find, because Las Vegas, where we were staying, was blazing hot. Finally, we saw our bus pull in and we headed over to it.

Once they found our names ("Waure") on the manifest, they informed us Dispatch wanted to talk with us. This is usually a bad sign. A lady got on the radio and told us our flight was overbooked, would we please take another one? In return, we would get a better deal, where we would be able to take a helicopter right down to the bottom of the canyon. Don looked at me inquiringly. I nodded yes, because the only way you will ever get me to the bottom of the canyon is to fly me down. I will never be able to climb the thing. So we merrily trooped back to our air-conditioned hotel room for a couple of hours.

Finally, the bus returned, and we were driven to the airfield. At this point I was still ok with everything. Then I saw we were going to take a prop jet to the Grand Canyon, on a flight of approximately 45 minutes. A prop jet. OK, how bad could that be?

Well, the short answer is, really bad. The plane flew low, and it was windy. The wind was causing the plane to do all kinds of things, the kinds of things that cause me to stay away from roller coasters. I tried gripping the seat in front of me. No good. My 13-year-old, who has no fear of planes falling out of the sky, tried to be helpful. "Calm down, Mom!" he would say whenever he would see my eyes widen or my knuckles whiten. He found repeating this did no good, so he let me hold his hand, using his other hand to pat me reassuringly on the arm. I have been assured that he will eventually regain full use of the one I was holding.

We landed near the West Rim of the canyon. I was nervous from the flight, but the people there reassured me that the chopper ride would be much smoother. It was. The only problem I had with it going down was I was stupid enough to look down into the canyon for about 4.4 nanoseconds, causing me some distress. Once we got down there, we were permitted to wander for about 10 minutes. I have to admit the view of the canyon from the inside went a long way to make up for the butterflies in my stomach.

After we flew back out of the canyon, we boarded a bus that took us to the edge of the West Rim, where we were served a light meal and permitted to walk around. I was nervous here as well because this part of the canyon has NO rail. I was assured by the bus driver that there had been no accident since this part had been open to the public in 1987. Big deal. I am a mom, and part of my job is to worry about my kids, who make mountain goats look clumsy, falling off the edge.

My solution to this was to remind them to "be careful" about 2,343 times and not look when they climbed on stuff. I am happy to report that we all survived the experience, and the Grand Canyon is a great place to visit, and a sight that should not be missed. So don't hesitate to take a plane tour of the canyon! Remember to bring a hand to clutch for the flight over.

TWO WEEKS OUT OF THE LOOP

Some of you may have noticed that I've been nowhere to be found in Highlands County for the past couple of weeks.

No, I didn't make good on my occasional promise to run away from home. I haven't gone into the Witness Protection Program. And I wasn't holed up in my house exploring the finer arts of video gaming.

I was, truth be told, in Oregon. Lincoln City, to be precise. I, along with 15 other writers, was spending two weeks in an intensive writing workshop, aptly called The Master Class.

This isn't a workshop for the casual writer. Each of us had to carve out two weeks from our lives and responsibilities. It cost a chunk of change, not including actually getting there (one student came from England). Each of us demonstrated a hunger to pull our craft to a higher plane. And just enough craziness to stick with this business.

We pretty much took over the Anchor, a small hotel in Lincoln City. The place is amazing, with collectibles all over the place and a staff that worked hard to spoil us rotten. It was our home away from home for two weeks, and happily a pleasant one.

So you have sixteen writers, four instructors, and near the end of the whole thing, two New York editors. Other writers and a bookstore owner who drifted in and out. What happens in those circumstances?

Well, for sure there was some craziness. For example, your humble columnist managed to set off the smoke alarm in her room with a really steamy shower. Fortunately, one of the female staff was able to disconnect it before I deafened everyone on my floor.

Then there was "The Game," sort of a role-playing activity that allowed us to live around seven years of a writer's life. Many things happened to us due to a part of the game called "life rolls," which simulated incidents that might befall one in the writing life. One student had enough car accidents to be nicknamed "Crash;" a couple of people got hit with divorces, I had a house burn down.

Not all of the rolls were bad. I sold a bunch of short stories. One person got what was called the "Dan Brown roll;" a mega bestseller that made him a ton of money. The point was to give us a glimpse of how the writing life ran, the good and bad.

Besides the game, we sat in lectures. Lectures about writing. Lectures about the publishing business. What works – and what doesn't. And how we could get a little further down this road called the writer's life than we were.

And we wrote. We all wrote a total of three short stories while there, one of them a minimum of 10,000 words. Another story assignment (not the 10,000 word one) was given to us with less than 24 hours' notice. We also had exercises working on craft issues, learning tools that would improve our stories and novels.

So, after two weeks of intense work, stress, and not enough sleep, what did I get out of it?

I have a better understanding of my strengths and weaknesses as a writer. I have several short stories that will soon be in the mail. I have ideas for at least 3 new novels to write over the next few months.

And, I have confidence that I have two things needed to make this writing thing work. One is talent. The other? Drive. Keeping on keeping on even when it's tough.

The two weeks at a Master's Class student were life-changing and unforgettable. Stay tuned to see the results from them.

ALOHA!

As I type this column up, I sit at the tiny desk in Don's and my cabin aboard the Norwegian Cruise Line ship *Pride of America* as it makes its way to the island of Hawaii, our next stop on our tour of the Hawaiian Islands.

This trip is a gift to ourselves to help celebrate our 40th wedding anniversary. Readers with good memories will recall that anniversary was in January. We'd decided for various reasons to postpone our trip until now.

Getting here from Florida wasn't easy. We went from Orlando to Austin, Texas, which wasn't too bad. Then we got to our next stop: San Diego. After arriving, we dutifully searched for our flight to determine which gate we needed to be at, except we couldn't find it on the Departure board.

When we checked with an agent, we were informed that our gate was in another concourse and that we'd have to leave the secure area and go through security all over again to enter the next concourse.

This complicated things. You see, Don is a man who loads his pockets (and with cargo pants, we're talking about a LOT of pockets) the way a woman will cram everything into a purse. Getting them unloaded is a production.

Well, we had no choice, so we gathered our things and did the whole security bit again. Overall, San Diego isn't one of my favorite airports currently. But we did finally get on a plane and fly off to the island of Oahu.

Hawaii requires some adjustment. It's a six-hour time difference between Florida and Hawaii, which meant for us we got in at about 10:50 pm local time which our bodies treated as 4:50 in the morning. "Tired" doesn't begin to describe how we felt.

That was four days ago – I think. One thing about being on vacation is you lose your sense of time. But now my body at least is all confused about when we sleep and stuff and I've tried to appease it with random naps here and there.

But we've not just been trying to straighten out our sleep cycles. We've been enjoying Hawaii – and trust me, there's a lot to enjoy.

It would be impossible to tell everything we've done so far in this one column. But at least I can hit some highlights:

Saturday, we toured around various places in Maui, where I got my first taste of Pineapple Whip. Tasty and sweet is my verdict, though those scooping it out were overgenerous and Don had to help me finish it off.

At the end of the tour, we were giving a fresh pineapple. It smelled wonderful but Don and I had no clue what to do with it. We certainly didn't have the tools ourselves to open it, and no one at the hotel we stayed at or the cruise ship were inclined to help us out.

Sunday the preacher form the Maui Church of Christ picked us up at the dock and brought us to worship service. We immediately gifted Corey and his wife Ashley with the pineapple we'd gotten. Ashley kindly cut it up and made it available to all of us in attendance. It tasted as good as it smelled.

Sunday night we watched a fantastic sunset over a volcanic crater. The only thing that marred the experience was that it was at 10,000 feet elevation – and the two Floridians didn't realize however nice it had been at sea level it would be cooler at the crater.

I braved the cold in my t-shirt and snapped some pictures of the sunset. Then I hurried back to the warm bus. Next time we'll know better.

I could write more, but I'm already over my wordcount. Come back next week for part two of my vacation in Hawaii. Aloha!

MORE ALOHA

Last week I discussed the first few days of our Hawaiian vacation. We were gone for nearly two weeks so believe me when I say there is a lot to cover. And it's a challenge, because the days tend to blur together, so my tale may not be chronological.

The ship itself was comfortable. Instead of assigning us to a dining table and time, the ship practiced what was referred to as "open dining." That meant places included with our passage and were open when you were hungry, let you pick a spot to sit and enjoy your meal.

Cruise ships, at least in my experience, have good food. Don and I usually went to the buffet place for our onboard meals, and we quickly fell into a pattern. We would locate a table and I would guard it while Don got me coffee (breakfast) or juice (other meals). He would then load up his plate and when he got to the table it was my turn.

They had a variety of choices. I discovered their Eggs Benedict and had more of that than was good for me. Lunch and dinner varied depending on what was available. But both Don and I ate enough to gain more than a couple of pounds. It was worth it.

Three times we went to one of the specialty restaurants on board. This was part of a package we bought, and we quickly discovered that drinks other than water were not included. Fortunately, the water wasn't Sebring water.

When not on the ship we went on excursions exploring the various islands. I hate to admit this, but in my opinion, Hawaii is prettier than Florida. The scenery is lush and we discovered a number of beautiful spots as we traveled. Our van would turn a corner and you'd suddenly see a waterfall as you passed by. Or maybe a brilliantly colored plant (I can't remember all of them, but they were lovely).

One tour we did took a mildly comedic turn. In the middle of the tour we were served a picnic lunch at a couple of tables under a tree. All was well – until it started raining. We'd encountered rain several times on the trip but not during mealtime.

Fortunately, the guide had umbrellas ready to use and we managed to finish lunch with a minimum of sogginess. Everyone was a good sport about the weather and we just counted it as a part of the trip.

One challenge I faced was on our next to last stop before returning to Honolulu. The port was too small for the ship to dock, which meant to get to land you had to get on a smaller boat, called a "tender." This meant you were on a vessel moving up and down in the water trying to step on another vessel moving up and down in the water.

I do not have good balance and doing this was the most terrifying thing about the trip. The crew was patient and understanding, and I managed to get on and off the thing without falling into the water, which says more about the expertise of the crew than my own skills.

We were on the ship seven days. One thing we did the day we got off the ship was visit the Pearl Harbor Memorial in Honolulu. We took a trip to the *USS Arizona* memorial, a place that was quiet and somber. Over 900 men are interred in the ship, which you can see a portion of through a hole above the ship.

We then got to the *USS Missouri*, where the Japanese surrender in 1944 took place. It was interesting if a little challenging since you had to climb quite a few steps to get to it and getting off from the ship took time for me. But if you have any interest in history, it's a wonderful place to visit.

Aloha, Hawaii. You are beautiful and a wonderful place to visit. Maybe, someday, I'll come back.

THE LONG WAY HOME

Recently I was in Oregon for my annual writing workshop. As usual, I flew there and back, this time on American Airlines.

Before I get into my traveling adventures, let me say the trip was productive. I sold a short story, connected with old friends, and made new ones. I also had a mini-meltdown and ate almost a whole pint of Ben and Jerry's Half Baked ice cream (hey, it happens). I also got the idea for a neat project I will be pursuing later this year.

The trip was a welcome break from my routine and enjoyable. But come Monday, ten days after I'd left Florida, I was ready to come home. I missed Don. I missed Mom. I missed what we call winter weather in Florida, which is balmy on its worst day compared to Oregon (think cold and damp).

So the first leg of my trip occurred with no problems. Once I landed in Phoenix, Arizona, I was welcomed with a text message that stated my 1:55 PM flight to Tampa was now scheduled to leave at 3:00 PM.

Optimistically I told myself that would give me time for a decent lunch before I had to get on the plane. It would get me into Florida an hour later, but I figured I would still be awake enough to make the 2 ½ hour drive back to Sebring.

A little while later, the flight's time was switched to 3:30. I admit I became mildly concerned with that, wondering what was going on. But I tried to remain upbeat while searching for something decent to eat that didn't cost an arm and a leg. I eventually got a cheeseburger and sweet potato fries that merely cost an arm. Pretty good if a little pricy.

At some point I learned that my flight (or the crew assigned to my flight) was coming in from New York, which had been experiencing worse winter weather than Oregon. Then, while at the gate, I got the bad news: the flight was further delayed until 6 PM.

This raised my concerns. My calculations quickly informed me that I would probably not get into Tampa until 11:30 PM or later. Throw in getting my luggage and finding my car, this meant I wouldn't even leave the airport until after midnight. And that was assuming American Airlines didn't give up and cancel the flight.

Let me quickly add that the staff in Phoenix were pleasant and helpful despite the situation. Even when we were redirected to another gate, they supplied us with apologies, sandwiches, and drinks.

I called Don and we debated whether I'd be able to safely navigate home at the late hour. Since I couldn't be positive about my ability to do so, not sure how tired I would be (I don't sleep well on planes) Don elected to get me a hotel room in Tampa. I would sleep some and come home Tuesday morning.

Happily, we did take off around 6 PM and got to Tampa after 11. I wearily gathered my luggage and tracked down my car. Armed with the address of the hotel, I plugged it into my GPS and braved city traffic.

The hotel...let's just say the location wasn't optimal. If we'd not already paid for it I might have either tried to drive home anyway or found another place. But despite the appearance of the neighborhood I was fine. After a few hours of sleep I managed to get home with no problem.

So look out, Sebring: I'm back. Hopefully, my next trip out of the state won't be so interesting. After all, there's only so much Ben and Jerry's I can eat.

SHORE LEAVE

A week ago Friday I got up much earlier than I wanted to in order to fly to Tampa International Airport. I was headed for Baltimore, Maryland, to a fan-run convention called Shore Leave.

Shore Leave is a convention (or "con") that is about science fiction and fantasy media in general and Star Trek in particular. It is an awesome place if you're a geek. While it isn't a writer's con, it does feature authors.

I should know that last. I was a guest author. You see, about ten years ago I was honored to have a Star Trek story published in the Pocket Books anthology *Strange New Worlds 10*. That one credit and my willingness to sit on some panels got me into the convention for free, though I still had to get there and pay for my room.

Getting there was...interesting. I flew to Baltimore on Spirit Airlines, which is supposed to be inexpensive. What they don't tell you up front is that if you have a carry on, you will be charged for it. If you want to select your seat, you will be charged for it. If you get thirsty on the plane and want something to drink, it'll cost you.

I grudgingly paid for my carry on (I had no checked baggage) but let them assign me a seat and decided I wouldn't die of thirst on the flight. I managed to score a window seat and TSA pre-approval so it wasn't all bad. I'm just not sure I'll fly them again with their extra costs.

Once there, I had to find my way to the hotel, a good half hour away. Having lived in small communities for so long I was unsure about the protocol when it came to taxis. Fortunately, several were lined up when I came out the door and one very comfortably took me to the hotel.

The price was a case of sticker shock. I really don't use taxis that much.

Once there, I made my way to registration, where I found a nametag with my name printed on it and a white ribbon under it saying, "Guest." I was expected. That cheered me.

I didn't have a lot of time, since my first panel occurred less than two hours after I arrived. I quickly changed into my Princess Leia t-shirt (the closest I came to a costume) and hurried to the meeting room.

I served on seven panels over Friday and Saturday, attended one or two more, and generally had a good time. I met with old friends and scored a couple of new ones.

Where there people in costumes there? Absolutely. One person was walking around dressed as Darth Vader from Star Wars, complete with theme music. A huge T-rex shared an elevator with me. There were really too many costumed folk to count.

A couple even got married at the convention. I didn't attend the wedding but did stop in at an open reception which included a cake shaped like a starship. Only at a con.

But a good number of people were like me, dressed in normal clothes, looking like someone you might pass on the street. Geeks may seem crazy on the inside, but outside we can easily pass for normal. Hope that doesn't frighten any of you.

All in all, it was a great weekend and I got home to find the place was still standing. I came back with a few souvenirs (not as many as you might think, given my limited suitcase space) and a lot of good memories.

Don't be surprised if I return next year. If you want to feed your inner geek you're welcome to come along. We'll drink Diet Cokes and swap stories. Just let me know if you're wearing a costume. I might want a picture.

THE LAST ROAD TRIP

I kid a lot about being crazy. In one sense, there is some truth to the statement. I'm a writer and any artist tends to see the world differently than others. So yes, I am a touch crazy.

But in our day to day lives, Don and I tend to be sane individuals. We rarely do things that cause friends or family to raise their eyebrows or express concern. We can usually be counted on to not commit actions that on their surface are not quite normal.

Last weekend, Don and I chose to do something insane.

A young man living with us named Mike wanted to move to Joplin, Missouri to live with his mother. He couldn't get there on his own, for reasons that I cannot get into. He needed help making the trip.

Don and I decided to help. Our plan was to rent a minivan, load it with Mike's stuff, and drive him and our bird Josie (Mike and Josie loved each other and we didn't want to separate them) out to Joplin.

So far, this doesn't sound TOO insane. Here's where the crazy clicks in:

Don didn't want to take time off. So, we decided we would leave on Friday afternoon, drive about half the 18-hour drive, find a hotel, and sometime Saturday deliver Mike to his new home. We would then head back to Sebring, with the goal of arriving back in town in time for Don to see patients on Monday morning.

People who are experts at long-distance driving are probably shaking their heads in dismay. The rest of you are asking yourselves what were we thinking?

Yes, we are both sixty-five. But Don had faith we could pull this off. I was concerned, but figured if we pushed ourselves we could get it done and I'd have Monday to collapse.

The trip started all right. Don managed to get home early and so we got to a good start. We eventually hit Georgia and had plans to get as far as Columbus before we quit for the night.

The minivan had other ideas.

It was my turn behind the wheel. We'd just filled up with gas and I started the vehicle, only to be greeted with a low tire pressure warning. This is not what you want to see at night in a strange town.

Don and Mike tried to put air in it, and then discovered that a screw had lodged itself into the tire. We realized that we weren't making it to Columbus that night.

Unfortunately for us, a marathon was taking place that weekend in Albany. We managed to find ONE hotel room to share and crashed for the night, hoping things would improve on Saturday.

Saturday morning, we found a tire place. Fifteen minutes and $10 later the tire was plugged and we were once again on our way to Joplin. But we were behind schedule and there wasn't a way to make up lost time.

In fact, just because Nanny (our GPS) said the drive was eighteen hours long doesn't mean it was eighteen hours long. This did not include stops, traffic, or any other delays. When all was said and done, we didn't arrive at Mike's new home until after midnight.

Don and I stayed in Joplin that night and did our best to power through the hours to get back by Monday morning. Unfortunately, the spirit was willing, but the flesh was weak. Even though we tried to minimize breaks (and spent a grand total of three hours at a hotel to take the edge off) we didn't get back into Sebring until nearly one in the afternoon. Don wound up cancelling patients for the day.

When we got home, we looked at each other and vowed, "Never again." We now know our limits. From now on, no more long road trips. If we are going somewhere a good distance away, there are airports.

I'm sure we'll find other ways to be crazy. Stay tuned.

RANDOM STUFF

We close out the collection with columns I didn't feel fit in any of the other categories. These columns cover many topics, from boneless wings to Star Trek conventions, Hurricane Irma to firemen not afraid to get their nails painted.
Get ready for a fun read.

BEING KIND

It seems as if every day we're getting slammed with bad news. Often said bad news includes people behaving badly to one another.

This is a shame. If ever there was a time we should pull together as a people, 2020 should be it. With all we're dealing with, doesn't it make sense we try to face it in a united front? Or have we just gotten used to battering each other, often for the offense of not agreeing with us?

This is depressing. So, for this week's column I sought out people who dared to be different. People who reached out to others in kindness instead of vitriol. I figured that maybe some positive examples could inspire us all to be the same.

The first story takes us to Alaska and something called "the Venmo Challenge." According to the article I read on www.foxnews.com, the challenge apparently involves people on social media asking their followers to donate to a Venmo account. When the account gets a lot of money, the owner of the account takes the money and goes to a restaurant, where they surprise their server with a huge tip.

Let me pause my tale here and acknowledge that people working in the food service industry haven't had it easy these past six months. Some restaurants closed down altogether. Some opened with limited seating and hours. Many workers saw their hours cut and less contact with customers, which affected their tips.

Angelina Backus, who works at Midnight Sun Brewing Co. in Anchorage, had no idea what was going on when she was told one of her tables wanted to speak with her. To her utter surprise, a man at the table took out his wallet and presented her with five $100 bills.

Backus was stunned and admitted that the gesture was "very special."

The article further states that the Venmo Challenge has grown in popularity in recent months. I think it's a lovely thing, though I really would want to know someone before I donated money to something like this. But still, the idea has a lot of merit and is kind to those who need it.

My other story about being kind involves your humble columnist. One of the things I enjoy doing is taking myself out to eat from time to time. While I also like eating out with others, sometimes I'm perfectly happy to go by myself with only my phone or my Kindle for company.

I have several options here in Highlands County for dining. One place is Village Inn. I like Village Inn because the food is good, the people are nice, and I've become hopelessly addicted to their Caramel Pecan Silk Supreme Pie. I must restrain myself from going there more often because of that pie. I already have weight issues.

Anyway, I recently paid a visit to the restaurant. I'm there often enough that they know me on sight, if not by name. My waitress, whose name escapes me at the moment, chatted with me a bit. I don't remember all we talked about, but it was a pleasant conversation.

At the end of my meal I gave into temptation and ordered a slice of pie. When she brought it to me, she smiled and said, "I comped your pie." In other words, she wasn't charging me for it.

I was surprised. But then she said, "You're always so nice when you come in here."

If I were a participant in the Venmo Challenge, you'd better believe she'd have gotten all the money right then and there. Unfortunately, I couldn't give her a $500 tip. But I did make sure it was a good one.

Kindness. It can be a big deal. Try to find a way to show kindness this week to someone. After all, at some point you might need it yourself.

CARRYING OUR LOAD

L adies, do me a favor. Track down your pocketbook. Got it? OK. Now, what do you have in it? A recent and quick glance at mine revealed the contents therein included and were not limited to:

  – A wallet and credit card holder

  – A planner I keep promising myself to coordinate with my computer organizer.

  – My cell phone

  – A Zip disk I carry in the unlikely event I get all my work done at church and want to work on a column or play an online game.

  – Tictacs (spearmint flavor)

  – My confirmation letter for a convention I attended over a month ago.

  – A pamphlet on bear safety I got during our vacation over 2 months ago.

Depending on the size of your bag, your list may be longer or shorter than mine. My interest in this stems from a recent newspaper article that talks about handbags today. Since women have the reputation of carrying anything and everything in their bags, they are bigger than ever. Some women apparently are toting so much stuff around they have abandoned purses altogether and are resorting to backpacks.

In my day to day living, I would have a hard time with a small purse. "Speak softly and carry a big purse" is my motto. Big purses serve many useful purposes - you can carry a lot when you have to (or even when you don't have to), and in the event you needed to defend yourself are heavy enough to give someone a concussion.

I also only have one color for my everyday purse: black. I realize I probably violate about seven fashion rules with that preference - I think you are supposed to carry a white purse in the summer. But to me black comes with all kinds of advantages. A black purse goes with everything, including faded jeans. Black also doesn't show dirt very well, a big plus for me given the state of my car's interior.

Since I tend to carry a lot in a purse, it should come as no surprise that my everyday purse began to show some wear and tear. When one of the straps threatened to rip off, I decided it was time to embark on a search for a replacement. So I waited for the ideal time (kids in school) and went to the mall.

I checked out four department stores and found myself confronted with a staggering array of choices. I saw purses of all kinds of sizes and colors. I also saw backpacks and found myself grateful for the warning the newspaper article had given me regarding this fashion trend. I might have gone openmouthed in shock otherwise.

I had gone looking with a definite mental list of what I wanted in a purse. It had to be big; it had to be black; and I really wanted one of those organizer type purses.

By nature, I am not an organized person. This is why a purse that is the equivalent to a cloth bag would never work for me. I would drop everything into it in a jumble and become completely flustered searching in it at the checkout line for my wallet, which of course would have worked its way to the very bottom of the bag and be buried under 20 other items. To save myself such hassle, I try to get a purse that has places for everything, so that when I have to rummage through it, I only need to paw through a small section of the purse to find the item buried on the bottom.

Shopping for a purse can be difficult. If you are looking for a dress, you at least get a chance to try it on before you buy it. You have no such luck with purses. I would look at a purse, paw through its innards and wish I could pitch out all the paper that new purses are invariably stuffed with and start filling it with my old purse's contents, just to see if they would fit and be readily available. But then I would imagine the looks I would get from the salespeople, who no doubt have fun on the job watching women search through new purses and decided that I would just hang on to the receipt until I got the thing filled.

It finally came down to two purses. Both were organizers; and included different accessories. The one I finally decided upon included a makeup bag, a place for my clip on sunglasses, a wallet/credit card holder with its own shoulder strap, and a small umbrella that won't fit in it anymore now that I have filled the bag with my "essential" items. Oh, well.

I would like to close this column with a warning to my fellow purse-toters. As part of my research for this column, I decided to pay attention to people carrying purses in a store recently. To my dismay, I saw many of you plop your bag in the kiddie seat of your shopping cart. Worse, one of you had done that and was dragging it from the other end, your back to your pocketbook and any nimble-fingered thief that might have been about.

Guard your purses, ladies. There are people out there who might appreciate your taste in handbags just a little too much.

HONK IF YOU HATE LOVEBUGS

This is the time of year that all of us look out our windows and cry, "Oh, no! They're back!" They, of course, being those very unlovely creatures, the lovebugs.

In case this is your first September in Florida (or you are my spell checker that doesn't recognize the word "lovebug") let me explain. Lovebugs are those small black bugs you see flying around in ever increasing numbers this time of year. Often, you will see two of them hooked up together (hence the "love" part of the name). Many of these bugs die on the radiator grills, front hoods, and windshields of cars speeding down the highway, which makes car washes VERY happy at this time of the year, not to mention those who paint cars. Lovebugs HATE being smashed by cars and pay you back in death by eating your paint job with their body fluids.

I have yet to hear someone say something nice about a lovebug. Most people say "ewwww,"or "Yuck," or other things that I won't go into. As an exercise I decided to try to think of some nice things to say about lovebugs. After all, all living things want to be loved - besides, part of being a good writer is being creative. Anyway, here goes:

--Lovebugs are the great equalizer. They don't care if you are rich or poor, male or female, driving a Lincoln Continental or a beat up rattletrap - if it's a windshield, they will smash it. The same goes for light colored houses - they don't seem to care where you stand on the socio-economic ladder, if your house is a light color, they will swarm it.

Of course, I knew that when I chose light almond colored siding when we built this house. I never said I was smart.

--Lovebugs make sure that those who wash cars or paint them have continuing income to feed their family. I am not kidding about the damage a dead lovebug can do to car paint. Actually, a source tells me that ANY bug that meets its death through impact with a car will damage the paint job, but lovebugs compound the damage by sheer numbers.

So, what to do? You could wash your car every couple of days, but who has time to do that? And who WANTS to clean bug goop off their car? So, we race to the car wash and let THEM deal with the messy job, which makes them very happy. Or, if we want to save money, we do the job ourselves. Some people have actually used SOS pads on their cars to scrape the bodies off. This may not please the car wash people, but it THRILLS the paint job people, because using an SOS pad on your car is the equivalent of using sandpaper, and even LOVEBUGS can't kill a paint job like an SOS pad can. So, as you see how much all this painting and cleaning costs, you can comfort yourself in the fact you have contributed to the economic well-being of Highlands County.

--Lovebugs are a non-controversial topic of conversation. Everyone will argue about the political situation, what we should do about the roads, the weather, whether McDonald's or Burger King has the best fries - but what's to fight about concerning lovebugs? Everyone hates them. It's something even liberals and conservatives can agree on in lovely bipartisanship that would be beautiful to behold. Today, agree on lovebugs; tomorrow, the budget?

Finally, while I would not presume to speak for God, I have a theory as to why He gave us the critters in the first place: as payback for our great winters. Think of it. In the winter, we can run around here in short sleeves, having picnics and going swimming, while up

North, people are freezing their noses off. God, being a just God, may have looked down with pity on our Northern friends, and deciding things needed to be equalized declared, "Let there be lovebugs." (This is also the reason He gave us cockroaches the size of small dogs, but that's another column.)

You can say all kinds of things about lovebugs, but the best thing will be said around the end of the month: "Good riddance!"

CHRISTIANS IN NAME ONLY

I've been hearing a lot lately about Christians. Specifically, what a "true" Christian would or wouldn't do, or how a "true" Christian would or wouldn't act.

Most Christians (or people who claim to be Christians: more on that in a minute) at least pay lip service to the concept of doing what Jesus would do. After all, the very name "Christian" means "Christ like." As followers of Jesus, we are to imitate Him in the way we conduct our lives.

At least, that's the theory.

In order to imitate Jesus, we need to know how He would act in given situations. This admittedly takes some extrapolation, since Jesus, for example, never drove a car. Deciding what He would do when someone cuts you off on U.S. 27 means falling back on general principles. (In the example, for instance, I am certain He wouldn't cuss at the driver, given the way the Lord treated people in general).

Even though He never ran for public office I'm also pretty certain that if He did He wouldn't engage in lies, lies, and more lies in order to get votes. And once in office He wouldn't let campaign contributions keep Him from doing what was right.

I've heard people all over the political map claim that Jesus would do "such and such" that they happen to agree with. Some of the things suggested that Jesus would approve of make me wonder if the proponent actually read the Bible, or are they basing their idea of Jesus on their personal opinion?

I have been told that America retains a majority of Christians in its population. While I agree that a majority of Americans might identify themselves as Christian, I wonder how many of them are moving their lips rather than their hearts.

I even have a name for such: CINOs (Christians In Name Only). There are a number of people who are quick to say they follow Jesus – but it's only under their conditions and on THEIR terms, not His.

I'm not talking about someone who's sincerely trying to live by Jesus' teachings who messes up at times – we are all sinners. I'm referring to people who know what Jesus says about a given behavior or situation, and choose to either ignore His words, or worse, twist them to justify what they want to do.

"But Laura," you may be asking, "Can one really KNOW? Isn't the Bible flawed? And Jesus never spoke about (insert your issue here)."

Okay. Either you believe that a God who created something from nothing can make His will clear to us or you don't. If you don't, just out of curiosity, why are you following Someone you can't be sure about?

Jesus just doesn't speak from the red lettered words of His book. If you believe the Bible to be inspired, He speaks from every page. If you don't – well, again, why are you following it then? Why put your trust in something that isn't trustworthy?

Yes, to follow the Bible means taking stands that will be unpopular. Especially in today's culture, which wants to excuse any and every behavior a person can come up with. It means living life in such a way that may not win you friends. It means saying "No" to things the world commands you to embrace.

But if you're a CINO, none of that is necessary. You just have to talk the talk. Let the world decide your morals for you, not God.

Recast Jesus into your likeness, make Him soft and malleable, agreeable to your worldview.

I can't tell you what you are. Just one question: are you brave enough to look in the mirror through the Word and find out?

ONE MORE CHEER FOR THE BUCS

Ok, listen up. I am a Bucs fan!

Finally, after years of saying that apologetically, the way you would speak of a major character flaw, I can say that with a measure of pride. Finally, I can state my allegiance to the Tampa Bay Buccaneers without the fear that my audience would view me as stupid and/or insane. Finally.

Before we go much further in this column, I need to explain something. I am a Bucs fan - not a football fan. My understanding of the game is very basic: I know the object of the game is to get the football past your opponent's goal line. I know what a field goal is. I know the center crouches at the center of the front line and the quarterback is the boss. That's it. Stray too far from that basic information and I take on the confused, glazed look you might get if we were talking about Star Trek.

I first learned of the existence of the Bucs way back in 1977, when I began attending the University of South Florida in Tampa. Around that time I met Jimmy DuBose, who was with the Bucs until a knee injury sidelined him. I was Jimmy's friend, so it made perfect sense to me to support the Bucs.

Even after Jimmy was no longer with the team, there were reasons to support the Bucs. I have lived a number of years in the Tampa/ St. Petersburg area. The Bucs were our "home team." Even after moving away from the area, I had no strong motivation to change my mind, so I more or less continued to call myself a Bucs fan.

Not that it's been easy to be their fan. The Bucs have tested their fans faith a number of times over the years. So much so I felt a need to explain my preference. "I have a soft spot in my head for the Bucs," I would say, and people would smile understandingly. I would pay very little attention to the sports pages, and when I would hear the Bucs were out of the running (again), I would shrug and forget about it for a while.

Until this year. Then, suddenly, the Bucs were one game away from the Super Bowl. Most of the predictions I heard were pessimistic as to their chances. Still, this was the closest I'd seen them come, so I waited.

When I heard the news the next day I was surprised. And then excited. The Bucs were going to the Super Bowl! I called my Colorado sister.

"What does Abhi think about the game?" I asked. Ahbi is my 12 year old nephew who is a walking sports reference. If anybody could tell me Tampa Bay's chances, it was him.

"He says he thinks Tampa will win," my sister answered, no doubt amused at my newfound interest.

Thus, for the first time in my life, I found myself watching a Super Bowl last Sunday. I wasn't a fanatic about it; I did other things while the game went on, such as balancing my checkbook. But I watched and tried to understand what was going on as commentators apparently speaking in tongues told me what was going on.

However, in the end, it was obvious even to a football rookie like me. Bucs, 48. Raiders, 21. The Bucs had won the Super Bowl. For real.

So, I hold my head up high now. I am a Bucs fan. And I make no apologies for it.

Oh, and all of you who said you would quit smoking, go on a diet, take the kids fishing, or whatever, "When the Bucs won the Super Bowl?"

Pay up.

THE MYSTERY OF THE MISSING CHOPPERS

One of the creatures that are currently inhabiting the Ware household is an iguana. This iguana, named Quincy (after a cartoon iguana) is the pet and companion of my oldest boy, who keeps this reptile happy in his room in an aquarium.

I am not sure if Quincy is a boy or a girl. John is convinced that the iguana is a she. I have no idea how one would figure this out, and even if I did, I'm afraid it would mean getting a lot more up close and personal with the reptile then I would like. So, for now I will refer to Quincy as "she."

Anyway, John takes complete care of Quincy. He feeds her, bathes her, cleans her tank (when I nag him), and does a good job overall with her. Every morning, he chops up zucchini and squash, adds some red gunk and calcium, and poof! Breakfast. To do this, he employs a food chopper - one of those gizmos with a glass container and a chopping blade with a spring that you push until the food is at the desired consistency. If you have ever used one of these things, you know that others can tell how stressed you are by how hard you smack the plunger.

Anyway, this column concerns the fact that John recently broke his chopper. Yes, his. To spare my own chopper, I got him his own. A good thing, too, since John managed to break two of the four blades of his chopper. He immediately informed me that I needed to get him a new one.

No problem, I thought. How hard could it be to find one of these things? They are not exactly a specialized item. They are fairly common. They are even pretty cheap for a kitchen gadget.

Well, I have been to two stores so far, and have found empty spaces where these choppers would be. In one store, I could have spent five dollars more and gotten a different, more expensive kind of chopper, but this is a reptile we are talking about. The one employee I spoke with had no clue as to why these items should suddenly go missing.

This has sent my imagination racing. What could be causing an apparent (I haven't checked all the stores yet) chopper shortage in Highlands County? Is there something about Y2K preparedness that requires food choppers? Has everyone's choppers in the county broken simultaneously? Has there been a bunch of iguanas bought in the area and people are needing choppers to feed them? Have some parents snapped over their children's Pokémon addiction and are buying up the choppers to convert the trading cards into colorful confetti?

Of course, there are other solutions other than plunking down the money for a new chopper. I could surrender my very, very nice chopper, but then it would vanish from my kitchen, possibly never to be seen again. And I have gotten rather fond of it.

As an alternative, I could let him use my food processor. But anyone who has operated this machine knows how easy it is to reduce food into sub-atomic particles in them. Using the food processor would also invariably get me involved in feeding the iguana - a job I can live happily without.

Then too, he could just chop the food finer with a knife. But since he tends to ignore the perfectly usable cutting board that is on the counter and cuts the food wherever in the kitchen he happens to be at the moment (don't ask me why he does this; I'm sure it has some-thing to do with being nearly 13), more cutting means more risk to my nice countertops. (He doesn't know it, but if he keeps using my countertops as cutting boards he could well have an unhappy Christmas)

So the upshot is, I am going to have to take time out of my life and hunt down this common kitchen gadget in order to make sure my kitchen is a little safer from an adolescent who is determined, like any other adolescent, to drive his mother out of her mind. This gadget is out there, somewhere, and I will track it down sooner or later. Meanwhile, I hope my countertops will survive the mistreatment of my son as he strives to keep his reptile well fed.

BEING THANKFUL IN 2020

I f 2020 were a meal, I bet it would be liver and onions (if you're one of those strange people who LIKE liver and onions, substitute a hated food. Brussels sprouts, maybe). In any case, this has not been a year many of us have warm feelings about.

That makes this week a little challenging. As I type this, Thanksgiving is tomorrow. It's a time we're supposed to stop and count our blessings and remember what we are thankful for.

I've had to sit and think a while about this. It would be easy to be completely negative about the year. To say there's so much bad there can't possibly be any good to outweigh it. It really has been that kind of year.

But, to my delight, I've found some things. I share the following things I am thankful for in hopes that they will remind you of things you are blessed with. And maybe some of them will make you smile.

I am thankful that despite the things that have happened this year, God is still in control. Maybe you don't believe in God (go ahead and skip to the next point). Maybe you do but wonder why things are the way they are if He's in control.

Think of it this way. Think of riding in a car with someone driving you to a desired destination through unfamiliar territory in the dark.

You can't really see what's around you. And you might not have chosen this particular route. But you trust the driver knows what he's doing and will get you there safely.

That's what I mean about God being in control. I don't understand why things are as they are, and it's a little scary sometimes. But if He's driving, I'll know I'll get through it in one piece.

But I'm not just grateful for God – I am also grateful for two of the most precious grandchildren on the planet. And I'm grateful for their mother, who is generous on sharing pictures of them and even calling for a video chat every week so I can interact with them. Lavinia and Matthias are bright lights in the dimness that seems to permeate the year. I love being a grandmother, and I love them.

I'm also thankful for technology that has played a role in my staying in touch with friends and family. Yes, I gripe about it sometimes when it chooses not to work. But thanks to Zoom, for example, I can teach my Ladies Bible Class every week as well as stay in touch with fellow writers that I haven't gotten to see this year due to the pandemic canceling events.

And my family and friends are another blessing I should talk about. I am gifted with people who care about me. People who will pick me up if I fall. People who have seen my bad side and love me anyway. Such relationships are priceless, and I'm grateful for the roles they play in my life.

Finally, I'm thankful for the fact that the pandemic hasn't kept me from writing, though it did at first. At the end of June, I decided to write every day and haven't looked back. The writing has become a joy for me once again. And I'm thankful I can share it with others.

2020 has taken much from us. Let me urge you not to let it take away your joy. There are things in your life you can be thankful for if you take the time to consider them. I hope you find many.

SHOULD I CHICKEN OUT?

This week I'm going to express an apparently controversial opinion. I know this might offend some of you, but I feel strongly about this and given recent events I believe it's time to take a stand.

Ready? Okay...

I prefer boneless chicken wings to bone-in.

I have sampled bone-in chicken wings, and I find them somewhat lacking. I never seem to get enough meat off them. With boneless chicken wings, you get plenty of meat and often delicious sauce on them. Right now, I'm fond of Walmart's General Tsao's boneless chicken wings, found in their deli. They make a fine lunch.

But this leaves me at odds with a Lincoln, Nebraska man, who takes issue with the name, "boneless chicken wings." In fact, he feels so strongly about it he went before the Lincoln city council to argue that the name "boneless chicken wings" should be banished from their menus.

I am not kidding. Ander Christensen went before the council August 31st to make his plea. According to the article I read on www. fox13news.com (which includes the video that has since gone viral),

Christensen claims that the name "boneless chicken wings" is a lie, since there's no chicken wing material in the boneless version.

Christensen considerately put forward some alternate names for the boneless wings, which include "wet tenders," "saucy nugs," or even "trash." That last name I suspect reveals his opinion regarding boneless wings in general.

At the conclusion of his speech, after some light applause, one of the council members remarked that the young man was his son. I would love to have heard what father and son said to each other about this later, but that information was not included.

But there were responses to Christensen's plea. According to www.foxnews.com, both Omaha Steaks and the Nebraska Barbeque Council announced they stood with him.

On the other hand, the chain restaurant Buffalo Wild Wings admitted that while they respected his passion, they disagreed with his idea. Even so, they gave him free traditional wings for a year. In addition, they promised that for every boneless wing they sold on Labor Day, they would donate $1 to The Boys and Girls Club.

Christensen insists he doesn't want boneless wings removed from the menu; he just wants them renamed. He's vowed to fight on.

One of my first thoughts about this story is that things must be going pretty well in Lincoln, Nebraska for something like this to be brought up in a city council meeting. This is Christensen's biggest (forgive the word) beef? Not potholes or property taxes or any of the numerous issues that plague city councils across the fruited plain?

My second thought is while I'm as much for truth in advertising as anyone, calling these delicious foods boneless chicken wings is not the end of the world. Yes, they're closer in content to chicken tenders than chicken wings, but so what? For those of us who don't like bones in our food, they're an oasis.

Yes, I don't like bones in my food. I even buy boneless chicken breasts, which will dismay some who would urge me to buy bone-in and debone the thing myself. Believe me, I have tried to debone a chicken breast – the result is always a sadly mangled piece of meat on my cutting board.

But I'm a fair woman. If you want to call boneless chicken wings something else, knock yourself out. Call them wet tenders. Call them saucy nugs. I'd rather you didn't call them trash, but so be it. Just make sure you save me some. Honey barbeque sauce is a plus.

ABOVE AND BEYOND

Sometimes, it's very easy to believe that humanity is primarily composed of jerks and creeps.

Look at Washington, DC. Read or listen to the news. Scroll social media. You will find a number of examples of people behaving badly. Just be a woman playing the online game Words with Friends – I can't tell you how many times I've been hit on by some random guy in the game. I will even tell them I'm happily married, and it doesn't deter them (These days I don't wait. First comment that is the equivalent of "Hello, beautiful" and they're blocked).

Lest you conclude that it's hopeless out there, I want to share a story of two firefighters that went above and beyond the call of duty when it came to a little girl last October.

According to articles I read on Facebook, www.cbsnews.com, and www.apnews.com, two Utah firefighters responded to a car crash. North Davis Fire District Chief Allen Hadley and Captain Kevin Lloyd, both fathers of young girls, found one of the vehicles' occupants was a little girl who was unhurt but understandably quite upset.

The little girl was screaming and crying while medics checked out her mom, so the two firefighters took it upon themselves to try and calm the child. As a mom who has dealt with screaming and crying children, I know this is not an easy task.

They noticed that she was holding bottles of – of all things – fingernail polish. The men started talking to her about the polish and then – in what must have been a burst of inspiration – asked if she'd paint their nails.

Looking at their picture from the articles, these guys don't strike me as the type who regularly paint their nails. But apparently the request did the trick. It wasn't long before the little girl was calmly painting the guys' fingernails a bright purple.

None of the articles mention the child's age, but she must have been relatively young. There were pictures of the guys' fingers after she painted them, and my guess is she needs some more practice. Nevertheless, the guys even posed for pictures, purple polish and all.

There were great comments on the Facebook post about the incident. My favorite one so far was from a woman who wrote, "So pretty! You'll be glad to know we now have a LARGE bottle of polish remover in Dispatch for the next time."

These guys remind me that not everyone is bad. Their kindness and willingness to go the second mile is a fine example we should applaud.

Another example of good people? The other day I was bemoaning the fact that I would not see my latest grandbaby, born last month, until March. That may not seem like long to some of you, but to a grandma, that's an eternity to meet her sweet grandson.

One of my friends, a lady named Dixie, heard me and immediately suggested we go on a road trip to see Matthias, his sister, and their parents in South Carolina. I thought about it for a day and asked her if the offer was real. It was.

We leave for our road trip next Thursday. Stay tuned – I'll make sure to tell you all about it. And thanks to sweet Dixie who's willing to go above and beyond the call of duty for a friend.

MY KIND OF RACES

By the time this column sees print, the 12 Hours of Sebring will have passed into history. This is a great time for race fans in Sebring. "Welcome Race Fans" many business signs proclaim. As well they should. The 12 Hours is one of our few claims to fame that is known beyond our borders. That makes it a wonderful opportunity for Highlands County in general to show off, put on our good face and let people get a glimpse of what an exceptional community we are.

Look at what we have to offer. We have managed to maintain a small town flavor with big town amenities such as a mall. Now that the construction has moved on, US 27 is almost decent to drive on. The weather is neither freezing nor broiling at this time of year, and we've even been blessed with some rain to brighten things up. Aside from the chain restaurants, we have lovely places such as the Twin Oaks Tea Room and Dot's to dine in. And as a group, residents of Highlands County are nice folk to know.

I hope the above paragraph has buttered up everyone enough, because I now have a terrible confession to make. I am even a little afraid to admit this. But I am determined to be honest with my readers.

I am not a race fan. I am uncertain as to what will happen to me now that I have made this admission. Will some race fan run over my picture in protest?

Don't get me wrong, I don't hate racing. I don't think it is a bad thing. It just isn't something that excites me. Cars running around in circles at high speeds. I grant you, it's not something I could do without causing severe danger to life, limb, and property, but it's not something that fires my interest, either.

I don't know if I am the only one in Highlands County to feel this way. Maybe not. If there are others like me, those involved in the races might be interested in ways to attract us as well as traditional fans. I have come up with a few events that would go a long way to adding excitement to the races for me:

– The 10 Mile School Drop: Transport three kids to two schools that are 4 miles apart from each other and get everyone there on time in 15 minutes while obeying all traffic laws. In addition, at some point in the race the driver must simultaneously break up a fistfight in the back seat of the car and scrabble enough change off the car floor to provide lunch money to a third child.

– The 20 Bag Grocery Relay: The driver must transfer 20 bags of groceries from the back of a van with broken air conditioning on a hot summer day to a home, unpack them and put them away. The last three bags that can be unloaded must be filled with bags of frozen vegetables and at least 2 gallons of ice cream.

– The Cell Phone Scramble: Driver, while traveling at maximum allowable speeds, must find and answer a ringing cell phone that has fallen to the car floor and slid around. Once he has found the phone and answered it, he must maintain top speed and the utmost politeness while conversing with an aluminum siding salesman who won't take "no" for an answer.

– The US 27 Race: Must get from Lake Placid to Avon Park in the shortest amount of time. This would be an exciting competition, as the racer would not only have to deal with his competitors but also the following hazards: construction set up at random points with warnings posted a generous 100 feet away; traffic lights that sometimes refuse to turn green; trucks that think they are above all road laws; drivers who turn left while still in the furthest right hand lane; and people who ignore all speed limit signs and putter along at a comfortable 25 miles per hour. (Come to think of it, there are days I think we ARE running this particular race).

Well, I hope all you racing fans had a wonderful time at this latest 12 Hours of Sebring. Now, if you will excuse me, I need to go engage in a racing event that truly interests me - a race to the last piece of cheesecake in the house.

ONE PARTICULAR GRADUATE

I t's been a number of years since my youngest son graduated high school (I find myself bemused as I type that. Where did the time go?). While I of course rejoice with my friends as their kids graduate year after year, high school graduation is rarely on my radar anymore.

But then, there's this year. And Matt-man.

Matt-man is the name I gave my best friend's son, whose real name is Matthew. It's interesting to note that Matthew means "gift of God" and is also the name of one of the twelve apostles. Throw in the names of my two sons, John and James, and we've got a quarter of the apostles covered.

In many ways, Matthew is a typical teenager. He is obsessed with his electronics. He has favorite television shows. Occasionally, he drives his folks bonkers.

But in other ways, Matthew is far from typical. You see, when he was three years old, his parents received news that sent shock waves through them: their beloved only son was diagnosed with autism.

According to Tina, at the time it was the worst news she'd ever been hit with. She wondered if she could raise an autistic child. She might have had some questions for God about this particular curve ball in her life. And how would her child turn out?

Marriages have crumpled under less weight than this diagnosis. The road ahead for Tina and her husband Frank was uncertain. But they decided to hold hands and face it together, whatever happened. That alone is worth admiring.

They aren't wealthy people. But they did what they could for Matthew. Tina soon became his advocate, searching a maze of conflicting advice for what would be best for her son. She got herself educated.

It hasn't always been easy. I have at times received what Tina and I call "vent alerts," emails where we pour out the stresses in our lives. I've tried to be encouraging to Tina, though I have to admit I don't know what she's going through sometimes. (Side note: she has been there for me more times than I can count, despite her issues. One reason she's my bestie.)

I have watched Matthew not only grow but thrive from afar. While Tina and Frank have had their doubts about their abilities to raise an autistic child, Matt-man has grown to be a kind, loving person. He helps out at the congregation they are a part of (and kudos to that congregation for stepping up and including him.). He helps out around the house (though like other teens he occasionally has to be prodded.). While he is not capable of handling his own affairs (Tina and Frank recently were named his legal guardians since he's now 18) he is able to do quite a bit for himself.

And earlier this week, the day I typed up this column, Matthew walked with his fellow high school seniors and received his diploma.

It has been a long road. One filled with love, anxiety, and frustration. But Frank and Tina walked it with their eyes open, holding the hands of their beloved Matthew as they did so.

This fall Matthew will enter a program that will teach him life skills. He will still love his electronics and television shows. And no doubt at times he will still drive his parents bonkers.

But today, he achieved a milestone. One his parents weren't sure he'd get to. For that, I want to take a moment and tell the three of them, well done.

What? No, I am not crying. Some dust must've gotten in my eye.

IS IT A CHRISTMAS MOVIE?

T his week I am going to weigh in on a controversial subject. One that is hotly debated this time of year. One I have strong feelings about.

Is the 1988 movie DIE HARD a Christmas movie?

For the innocent, DIE HARD is an action/thriller movie starring Bruce Willis as a New York cop who gets caught in a Los Angeles skyscraper during a heist. The major bad guy is played by Alan Rickman, who would go on to play Severus Snape in the Harry Potter films.

The movie is rated R for language and violence. Made for $28 million, it would go on to gross $141 million worldwide in theaters. It launched Bruce Willis as an action hero and spawned four sequels. In 2017, it was selected for preservation in the United States National Film Registry.

The movie takes place during Christmas Eve, when off-duty cop John McClane (Willis) goes to LA to see his ex-wife and kids. He visits his ex-wife at her office Christmas party, taking place on the upper floors of the Nakatomi building. While there, German terrorist Hans Gruber and his crew crash the party, and McClane goes into stealth mode to try to save everyone.

There's a lot more going on than this sketch, but I don't want to spoil the movie if you haven't seen it. It's action-packed, and a thriller in every sense of the world. Lots of fun characters, lots of twists, and in and of itself a good movie.

Yes. Despite the language (which is one of the only issues I have with the film) and the violence, this is a good movie. I recommend it with the caveat that it won't be everyone's cup of tea, and definitely not for children.

All that being said, is it a Christmas movie?

There are those Scrooges who will point out it isn't about Christmas per se. It's about a cop trying to stop terrorists. It's an action film, therefore it's not a Christmas movie. And Bruce Willis is on record as saying it's NOT a Christmas movie, it's a Bruce Willis movie.

To all of them, even Willis, I say bah humbug.

The movie takes place on Christmas Eve, at a Christmas party. Christmas music is threaded throughout the score. It's also about a man trying to reconcile with his wife – a romantic element. One of the screenwriters of the film, Steven E. de Souza said in 2017 that it is a Christmas movie.

Furthermore, 20th Century Fox, who is behind the film, weighed in last year. On the 30th anniversary of the film, they issued a DIE HARD – CHRISTMAS EDITION that includes a movie trailer recut to present the film as a Christmas story. (The trailer is on YouTube and a hoot to watch.)

And in 2015, DIE HARD was voted the greatest Christmas movie by readers of the British film magazine *Empire*. Granted, this was one magazine and not American. But it's evidence for the point.

In case you haven't figured it out, I regard DIE HARD as a Christmas movie. It takes the holiday tropes and combines them with an action film. As a friend of mine pointed out, McClane's wife is named "Holly." That's just one of many details that point to the conclusion.

So, if you need a new holiday tradition, pour yourself a cup of eggnog, settle on the couch with a loved one, and watch DIE HARD. And if you want to challenge me about it, you can email me at laura@ laurahware.com. Just be prepared for a debate.

CAR TALES

Over the years I have owned or driven a number of vehicles. I still remember my first car, an old sedan with no radio and a drinking problem when it came to oil. I'd gotten it cheap and it did a fairly decent job of taking me where I wanted to go.

When I moved from Florida the first time, I sold the car to a friend of mine. My mother wanted to know what the poor girl had done to me to deserve that.

In time I've had my share of cars. Don and I together have owned a variety. We've had cars totaled in accidents. We had one car burn up in Texas (long story). We've managed to avoid lemons for the most part, even with Don's insistence that we stick to used cars when we buy.

Let me hasten to add that "used" does not mean "antique" – and we've wound up with good cars even without buying new. But there have been times I've driven a rental which is much newer than my 2006 Toyota (my current vehicle) and it has been a sweet experience.

One advantage of buying used, of course, is the price is much more reasonable. And as long as you have a good mechanic to look it over and make sure there's no nasty surprises, more often than not you wind up with a good car that will get you from Point A to Point B with no hassles.

I recently read on cnn.com that more Americans are behind in their car payments than ever before. According to the article, more than seven million loans are overdue by at least 90 days in the 4th quarter, says the Federal Reserve.

While that is a fraction of total loans in the US market – the total is about 89 million – it's a figure that's growing. People are having trouble making their payments, despite an economy that's improving.

Maybe that's what drove a Winter Haven, Florida man to drive a car off a dealership lot, claiming to take it for a test drive. However, he has as of this column not returned with the car, thereby incurring a warrant for his arrest.

According to an article on www.theledger.com, The Winter Haven Police Department issued a press statement detailing the incident. It claims that J'Briel Scurry, 29, and another man came to a Buick GMC dealership looking for a car on February 2nd.

Scurry actually was filling out paperwork for a vehicle he'd just test drove when the sales associate assisting him began helping other customers. Scurry and his pal went back to the lot and then asked for the key to a 2015 white Buick Verano so they could look at it.

When no one was paying attention Scurry drove the car away.

A short time later, someone noticed the vehicle and a dealership license tag were missing. The associate called Scurry, using the cell phone number provided on his paperwork. Scurry assured the associate that he was merely test driving the vehicle and would return it before the dealership closed.

That was the last anyone heard of Scurry. Subsequent calls to his cell phone went unanswered. A warrant was issued Monday for Scurry's arrest on charges of grand theft auto.

I wouldn't recommend this method to avoid car payments. If Scurry is caught he's going to have a lot more to worry about, though if he's convicted he won't need a car where he'll be going.

Hopefully you have a vehicle you can depend on and can afford the payments. And if you have a cool new car I can test drive, let me know. I promise I'll bring it back.

INSIDE A STAR TREK CONVENTION

L et's play a word association game. The words are "Star Trek Convention." What comes to your mind?

Did you think of people in weird costumes, geeks with pocket protectors, and people who just didn't seem quite right? Did you envision a room filled with pimply adolescents, speaking to each other in a strange language? Surely not something a mature woman with two children would go to, right? Well....

Let me start out by helping some of you out here. "Star Trek" started as a television show back in 1966 and has since spawned four additional series (the latest debuting later this month), a brief cartoon stint, nine movies, books beyond counting, and a merchandising empire. On the Internet, there are countless websites for "Trekkers" (term for the serious Star Trek fan) to peruse, as well as over 50 newsgroups on which to discuss things of a "Trek" nature.

It was on such a newsgroup that I first heard about a Star Trek Convention that was going to be held in Washington, DC in early August. DC was a tempting locale - I know people there, and it was close enough that airfare might be merely outrageous instead of out and out horrifying. So I entered negotiations with Don, hoping to get him to see how great it would be for me to go, and by the way, could I charge it to our credit card? Don, himself a Trek fan (though not nearly as obsessive about it as I am) decided he could handle the kids and the house for that period of time. The kids, who realized that my being gone left my computer free for their use, also supported the trip.

So early on a Thursday morning I found myself heading for Tampa International Airport, to travel to DC and engage in something most adults my age would deem frivolous, silly, and not worth their time or money. At the very least they would not admit doing such to close friends, much less a newspaper. But then, I seem to have these moments I do not act like most adults. This is to your benefit since many of you might be curious as to what people do at conventions but don't want to attend one yourself. Well, sit down, and I'll give you the highlights.

First, let's talk about the location. The convention was held at the fabulous Doubletree Hotel in Arlington, Virginia. Let me take a second here to explain my experience with hotels; I am the kind of person who, when traveling, tries to stay at one of those "family" motels. Places where if you get a continental breakfast in the lobby and a coffeepot in your room you count your blessings. The Doubletree is lightyears ahead of such places (pun intended). Thanks to a convention room rate, which was actually reasonable, I got to stay at the hotel, which meant I was 5 minutes away from the convention (that included waiting for the elevator) and I didn't need to rent a car, a blessing since I have so far managed to avoid driving in the nation's capital and want to keep it that way.

"Ok, Laura," you might be thinking. "They didn't hold the convention in a hole in the wall. But wasn't it WEIRD? What kind of people attend these anyway?"

Ok. Come closer. I will tell you the truth about what kind of people I saw at the convention. I hope you can handle the revelation. Are you ready? Most of the people at the convention looked like.....normal people.

I'm not saying that there weren't people in costume, because there were. Many wore "Starfleet" uniforms. In fact, I saw at least one baby in a uniform - he by far looked the best in it. But costumed attendees were definitely in the minority.

There were teenagers there, also. But a lot of adults, some even older than myself. Several younger kids were there with their parents. Most of them looked like people who you might see in the grocery store or the mall. Talking to them, they seemed as normal as I am - which in some people's opinion may not be saying much.

So what did I do during the convention? I bought some stuff from the dealer room, which had all kinds of Trek-related merchandise; I attended question and answer sessions with people who had acted or participated in one or more of the various Star Trek shows; I got autographs (probably the most "fannish" thing I did); took pictures, or at least tried to; and chatted with friends who, like me, had a love for the various series and wanted to talk about them.

In the end, at our final dinner together, we toasted the time we had enjoyed at the convention. Was it fun? Oh, yes. Could a normal person do it and stay normal? Well, maybe, but it would be an effort. Would I ever do something like that again? Given I see nothing so wonderful about being normal and after the great experience I had this time, what do you think? Would I recommend the experience to others? In the words of the Vulcan Mr. Spock, "It would only be logical to do so."

FLAG-WAVING

"Did you read Charley Reese's column in today's paper?" my friend asked me in an outraged voice.

I was forced to admit that not only had I not yet gotten to the morning paper, for all I knew it was still sitting on my front walk, waiting for someone to take pity on it and bring it in from the elements.

"You should see what he says about the flag!" my friend continued, obviously very ticked off. As she described the column, I could understand why she would be less than thrilled with Mr. Reese. I promised to look up the article in question when I got home that day.

When I finally got home, I found that the paper had indeed gotten inside the house. I picked it up and immediately turned to the column in question. I read it through, then decided to think about it for a while before forming an opinion about it.

In a nutshell, Charley Reese is upset with the proliferation of flags everywhere you look. On cars, in front of businesses, on jewelry - it is hard to go anywhere and not see the red, white, and blue in some form or fashion.

Reese feels this cheapens our national symbol. He would give the federal government exclusive use of the design of our flag. He would forbid commercial establishments from ever flying it and would only permit civilians to fly it on certain national holidays. As the title of his article puts it, "familiarity breeds contempt."

He is quick to dismiss the argument that the current flying of our flag is a show of patriotism. He cites the lack of attendance at Memorial Day services as proof that many Americans are not all that patriotic. "Anybody can fly a flag," he states. He further argues that flying the flag while we are at war is not true patriotism.

Reading the column several times, I understand why my friend was disturbed. And while I understand that Reese probably thinks he is upholding the flag with his arguments, I have to take issue with his recommendations and his conclusions.

One thing he states that I do agree with - using the flag as a marketing tool is wrong. I also dislike commercials around President's Day that use Washington and Lincoln to peddle someone's wares. Never mind that shopping, a boring necessity to guys and a recreational sport to gals, has now been deemed a patriotic activity. This use of our country's symbols does fall under the category of disrespect, and those engaging in it ought to know better.

But does Charley Reese really want to tell Americans it is wrong to display the symbol of our country? To demand that they not fly the flag except at certain times the government dictates? To criticize them for displaying it on their cars and in front of their homes? He goes too far with those attitudes in my opinion, and completely misses the point of all the flags.

One of the most touching images to come out of 9/11 was one where, in the midst of the destruction of the World Trade Center, an American flag waves brightly. There it stands, a symbol of our endurance in the face of terrorism. Would Reese decry this?

Yes, the flag is seen everywhere. I don't find that seeing it wave from a car's antenna, or pinned on someone's shoulder, cheapens its meaning for me. Instead, it fills me with a feeling of solidarity with my fellow citizens. What these flags say to me is that whatever faults we believe this country has - and there is not an American today that believes this country is perfect - we are united against those who would try to harm us. It is like brothers and sisters in a family - they might be able to fight and pick on each other, but woe to the outsider that tries to tangle with one of them - he will wind up facing the whole gang.

Look, Mr. Reese. It has been declared Constitutional to burn our flag in protest, an act that to me shows the ultimate disrespect for it. Do not go after those who wish to show their support of their country by flying it on their cars or in front of their homes. It is the least a patriot can do.

THE GREAT CAKE CAPER

It all started with my mother-in-law's birthday. She turned 89 last week, and as is traditional in the Ware household, we planned to have a cake. Ordered from a bakery.

Now it is true that I am capable of baking a cake. I have even done so in the past. Don sometimes wants something strange for a cake, like blue raspberry and cherry layers, and I am crazy enough to try and accommodate him.

My creations turn out okay, if a little lopsided sometimes. And I always need more icing then one can provides (yes, I use canned icing instead of making my own. I never claimed to be Martha Stewart). They are edible, if not pretty, and that's all my husband cares about.

But I have to admit it's easier on me if we order a cake, so Don went to Publix and after a phone consultation with Mom ordered a chocolate cake with raspberry filling, to be picked up on her birthday.

The night before Mom's birthday Don asked if I would mind picking up the cake for him. I said no problem, figuring I could squeeze it in with other things I had planned.

This is because I cannot see the future. Had I been able to, I would've definitely said no way.

My original plan had me picking up the cake on my way back

from Winter Haven, where I had to run an errand. Because life got in the way, I ran out of time for that and decided I would pick up the cake after Mom's hair appointment in the afternoon.

So I drove Mom to the hairdresser and killed time while she got beautiful for her birthday. Then we went to Walgreens on the south side of Sebring before heading to the Publix on the north side to pick up the cake.

Only when I got there, they couldn't find it.

After a flurry of confusion I suddenly remembered that Sebring is the proud owner of two Publix stores. A quick call to Don confirmed that I was in the wrong one, that the cake was at the Publix on the south side of town, where I had been moments ago.

Once that was straightened out I hopped back into my car and drove to the correct store. The cake was waiting for me there. I made admiring noises at it (it was pretty) and carried it out to the car, sure that our adventures were done.

I was not that lucky.

After Don got home my honorary son Paul and I were getting ready to pick up pizza for dinner for everyone except Mom, who wanted chicken. I asked Don if he needed the order form for the cake, which I still had.

He said he needed the receipt.

What receipt? Hadn't he paid for the cake when he ordered it?

Well, it turned out that's not how it works, and I had basically, if unknowingly, shoplifted a cake.

Because I am a Christian and an honest person, I couldn't let that stand. So this meant that Paul and I headed back to Publix with order form in hand, confessing my error and wanting to pay for the cake.

It wasn't that simple. They didn't have a barcode to scan. I hadn't brought back the cake which had the desired barcode.

No, I didn't have to go get the cake. Someone at the store figured out how to key it into the register and I paid for the cake, no longer a thief.

But all's well that ends well. Mom enjoyed her birthday and

claims that the cake is the best she's ever had. So it was worth the adventure to get it to her.

But be smart. If your loved one orders a cake and then asks you to pick it up, do what I should've done – tell them to get it themselves. Or at least make sure you wring all pertinent information from them, like where the cake is and did they pay for it?

As good as a cake might be, it's not worth a criminal record.

NEVER JUDGE A BOOK BY ITS MOVIE

I am currently in Oregon, attending a writing workshop. The dress code here is jeans and casual shirts. I enjoy bringing various t-shirts to wear under warmer stuff (Oregon is COLD at this time of year).

It's fun to compare my shirts with those of other writers since several of us have a fondness for shirts with cool pictures or sayings on them. One of the ones I wore this week made a simple yet profound statement: "Never judge a book by its movie."

As you can imagine in a group of over 50 writers and editors, the t-shirt was met with general agreement. Such agreement is not universal. My friend Kevin considers such a statement to be akin to blasphemy, since he is an avid movie goer and doesn't usually crack open a book. It is interesting to note that his wife is one of my biggest fans and reads anything and everything I write. Despite Kevin's mistake, she still loves him.

But I got to thinking about the statement and my experience with movies versus books. Admittedly some movies have led me to books. Years ago when I saw the trailer for the movie "The Hunger Games" it intrigued me enough to pick up the book. The book was good enough I binged through the entire series and sat through the movies, which were good for what they are but not as good in my opinion as the books.

Movies don't always try to stay true to their source material. There was a marvelous movie called "The Prestige" that starred Christian Bale and Hugh Jackman that came out a number of years ago. I eagerly got my hands on the book, only to find out it was nothing like the movie that it was the source material for. While I didn't hate the book, I will admit I enjoyed the movie more (Don't tell Kevin).

One series of movies that tried to stay close to the books was Peter Jackson's "The Lord of the Rings." Now you have to understand that I am a big fan of the books. Like many, I eyed Jackson's creation with some trepidation. How would it go?

I have to admit that for a bookaholic like me, the movies work. Jackson's choices of actors was spot on as far as I was concerned because they didn't clash with the images in my head. He kept in MOST of the important scenes and didn't take as many liberties as he might have. While it is impossible to please everyone, he managed to satisfy a good number of fans of the book.

Last week I talked about "Wicked" and how I had issues with the book while I enjoyed the musical. This is an example of it being dangerous to judge a book by another medium – in this case, a musical. If you saw the musical and expected the same tone in the book, you would come away sadly disappointed.

Part of the problem, of course, is you are discussing two different mediums when it comes to books versus movies. One is visual. The other requires you to make up your own pictures as you go. Movies have a limited time to tell their stories and often must cut things from a book so the film comes in at a decent running time (unless you're Peter Jackson and make films that can last days).

But I think, whether you love them or hate them, it is dangerous to judge a book by the movie based on it. Maybe someday we will test this with a book of mine. I'll let you know.

WHEN GOOD STORY MEETS BAD THEOLOGY

I admit that I went to see the latest "Left Behind" movie with a few preconceived notions. I'd read the books a long time ago, and I had a general idea of how the story was going to go. Still, I was curious to see how closely they stuck to the written word, and besides, I like Nicholas Cage. So off I went.

Let me say that the movie was entertaining. It had excitement, suspense, and as I said, Nicholas Cage. It covered only the first few chapters of the book by the same name, but you didn't feel cheated in the end. No word on if a sequel is planned, though there is still a lot of material the producers could go through. After all, the series runs twelve books.

Cage plays an airline pilot whose wife is a believer while he is not. While flying to London and contemplating an affair with a stewardess, the Rapture happens, taking a number of passengers and the copilot. Cage must land the plane in difficult circumstances back in the United States while struggling to figure out what's going on.

Of course there were differences between the book and the movie. It seemed to me that some of those differences were due to the transition from a print medium to a visual one. None of the differences made me feel annoyed, though it's been a while since I read the books.

But one thing keeps me from endorsing the film. And I don't go into this lightly. I for one would like to see more faith-based films out there. It would be nice if I could recommend this one, but in good conscience I can't.

The reason? The theology behind it.

"Left Behind" postulates an event popularly referred to as "the Rapture." During the Rapture Christians are supposed to be caught up into Heaven, leaving behind all earthly things, including their clothes. (Yes, both the film and the book postulate we will be meeting our Maker completely naked. Do not go there.)

Those left behind (you see what they did there, don't you?) remain to endure seven years of tribulation, some of the darkest hours mankind will ever see. They will have a chance to accept the Gospel during this time but will endure intense persecution if they do.

What's my problem with this? The people who promote this particular brand of theology come to it by taking Bible verses out of context and treating symbolic language as if it were literal.

People who buy into this tend to go to the book of Revelation to back up their points. Revelation isn't an easy book to understand. I've read it, even attended a class or two on it, and to say I completely get it would be misleading.

But I do know that most of it has nothing to do with modern times.

How do I know that? Let's go to the beginning of the book, Revelation 1:1: "The Revelation of Jesus Christ, which God gave unto him, to shew unto his servants things which **must shortly come to pass;** and he sent and signified it by his angel unto his servant John:" (KJV, emphasis mine).

In case you missed it, the things revealed to John were to "shortly come to pass." Not 2000 years later – shortly. The letter was written to Christians enduring horrible persecution who needed encouragement. How would it help them to know what would happen long after they were dead?

Unfortunately, I don't have time to go into more detail about my issues with this teaching, but I do want to make one final point. In Matthew 24:36 Jesus states that no one knows when the judgment is coming except God the Father. To say we can predict it by "signs" makes Jesus out to be a liar.

That's one of a number of false teachings I don't want to be a part of.

DEAR ANN LANDERS

L ike most of you, until a few months ago, I was a avid reader of Ann Landers and her sister, Dear Abby. The columns evoked different emotions depending on the contents. Sometimes I felt a crazy kind of relief, seeing other people had problems far worse than mine. Sometimes, they were funny. Sometimes, they were insightful. Sometimes, they were maddening, especially if I felt Ann was totally off her rocker in some reply she gave. Sometimes, they were just sad.

I admit I had stopped reading her and Abby several months ago. A lot of it was an issue of time - I hardly seem to have time to read the newspaper anymore and found myself skimming the advice columns if I looked at them at all. Still, I was stunned when Don came into my office and told me that Ann Landers had passed away.

She was born Esther Lederer, but to us she was Ann Landers. She and her sister were the advice ladies, the people you could write to about almost anything. And did we write. Ann was getting upwards of 2000 letters a day, even without an email address.

Even though there were many areas we probably didn't agree on, I confess I admired Ann for a number of reasons. She was smart. She was courageous, not afraid to say what she thought. She came up with one-liners that I, as a writer, would love to have thought of first. In fact, I still use one that she wrote in her very first column, answering a letter from a guy who had fallen in love with a lady he WASN'T married to: "Time wounds all heels."

As I think about it, to my astonishment, I find she was like me in many ways. She was a night owl, staying up until 2 AM and sleeping in the mornings, a lifestyle I would love to copy if I only could get away with it. She genuinely cared about people, as I do. She initially had trouble separating herself from the problems people wrote about - she had to remember these things were happening to them, not her. I'm still trying to learn this lesson, but she had more years to practice then I have had so far.

I also think that she wasn't afraid to be silly. There is no other explanation for what I remember as "the great toilet paper debate." A question was raised on how toilet paper should be hung in a bathroom: should it come over the top, or down close to the wall? Many people sent letters arguing pros and cons of both sides of this issue, and they were duly published in the column. To mature, rational human beings, such letters would be a waste of space. To me, as one who has a silly streak to assist me in my lifelong resistance to sanity, and I suspect, to Ann Landers, the whole thing was a joyful hoot.

I've read a lot of articles about her since learning of her death. Many people have extolled her for the advice she gave and the issues she brought to light. I can't say that I've always agreed with her takes on the issues - I am very conservative and I suspect we would be on opposite sides in many debates - but I do think there is something she gave to people everywhere.

Ann was the national shoulder to cry on. For the price of a stamp, you could sing the blues and tell your woes to someone who would really listen. They wouldn't interrupt you or cut you off. You could get it off your chest and be done with it. Moreover, no one had to know who you were. It wasn't like a face to face encounter, and it wasn't a call in show where you'd have to worry that someone would recognize your voice. You could tell your tale of woe safe in anonymity.

And to top it off, you would get advice. Maybe you wouldn't agree with it, but it would be something else to consider. It might even make you smile. In these days of inflation, that's a lot to get for the price of a stamp.

THOSE SCAMMY SCAMMERS

As I've mentioned previously, we are a family that still possesses a landline in our house. We have reasons to do so, though I warn people to contact me via my cell phone if they really want to get a hold of me.

Most of the phones connected with the landline have Caller ID, which has proven to be useful. I can normally tell at a glance whether or not I want to talk to the person (?) on the other end of the line, and nine times out of ten I don't. So I let it go to our phone's voicemail, to check and delete at my convenience.

The reason for this is that even though I put us on a Do Not Call list ages ago, either my time there has expired or a bunch of those calling me simply ignore that. I get calls from people trying to sell me all kinds of things or trying to trick important information out of me. I can live without talking to those people.

Unfortunately, the phone in the kitchen doesn't have Caller ID, so if I'm right by it when it rings, I feel compelled to pick it up in case it's someone I actually need to talk to. Just recently I answered it and was greeted with, "Don't hang up! This is not a sales call!" Whoever it was then said something about dealing with my chronic pain. At that point, given I a) don't have chronic pain, and b) have never hinted to anyone I have chronic pain, I hung up.

Yes. I know it's rude to hang up on people. There was a time when I would not hang up on a caller, no matter how obnoxious. Unfortunately, I have found these people refuse to shut up long enough to give you a chance to finish a call politely. So I will say "I'm not interested, thank you," and hang up.

I have no problem with hanging up on recordings. This is not rude, as contrary to fiction, machines have no feelings to hurt. And life is really too short for me to listen to them try to pry my credit card number from me.

I don't bother answering calls from the Republican National Committee, either. First off, they really don't want to talk to me, unless they want an earful about why I left the party. What they really want is to talk to Don and try to get money from him. I could save them some time by telling them he isn't going to give them any, but I doubt they'd believe me.

(This is not to imply that the RNC runs scams. But I know the only reason they call is to ask for money. If there are other reasons, I apologize for my mischaracterization)

Now the scammers have another trick. They have found a way to spoof local numbers so it looks like they're calling from someplace local, or even a friend of yours. I actually had someone spoof my cell phone number on my cell phone. I admit I answered that one, because I was curious as to why my cell phone was calling itself. It was either a sales call or a scam, which annoyed me greatly.

Sometimes I want to suggest to these callers that they find other work. Surely they're qualified for a job besides one that gets you a lot of people hanging up on you, some of them being hostile. And if you're a scammer...for crying out loud, how do you sleep at night?

Please stop calling me, scammers and salespeople. You just wind up wasting our time and upping my blood pressure. Use the free time from not calling me to check the want ads. Who knows? You might find something to do you like better. And we'll both be happier.

ALSO BY LAURA WARE:

Column Collections

Laura's Look 1998-2000

Novels

Dead Hypocrites

The Silent Witness

Redemption

Two Weeks in Guyana

Seek and Ye Shall Find

Death on the Air

Short Story Collections

Decisions, Decisions

Five Female Gumshoes

Seeking Refuge and Other Bible Stories

Sorcery and Steel (with Azure Avians):

Sisters

The Amulet Keeper's War

Aftermath

Harbringers

Tempest

ABOUT THE AUTHOR

Laura Ware continues to write her weekly column "Laura's Look" which has run in the Highlands News-Sun for twenty-five years. She also writes fiction, both short stories and novels. Her latest novel is DEATH ON THE AIR. Her essay "Touched by an Angel" appeared in *Chicken Soup for the Soul: Random Acts of Kindness.* Check for news and sign up for her free newsletter at www.laurahware.com. Or email her at laura@laurahware.com

www.ingramcontent.com/pod-product-compliance
Lightning Source LLC
Chambersburg PA
CBHW022113080426
42734CB00006B/117